THE GAME OF INNOVATION

OF

A VISUAL GUIDE

**Conquer Challenges
Level Up Your Team
Play to Win**

By David Cutler

Contributions by Lance LaDuke

Illustrations by Patti Dobrowolski

Design by Cara Belloso Pinto

McGraw Hill

New York   Chicago   San Francisco   Athens   London   Madrid
Mexico City   Milan   New Delhi   Singapore   Sydney   Toronto

Testimonials

Zeynep Temel
Assistant Professor,
Robotics Institute,
Carnegie Mellon University

INVENTION

My Challenge:
Build a robot that emulates the movement of an ant.

On Our Approach to Gamifying Challenges
I may just have discovered the secret sauce to innovation! This book showed me how "a-ha moments" result from focused efforts that set the stage ambitiously. I look forward to witnessing my own team's transformation, achievements, and unforgettable experience after following guidelines presented here. We are playing this GAME to win.

Felipe Buitrago Restrepo
Minister of Culture,
Colombia

GOVERNMENT

My Challenge:
How might we reignite our national cultural sector following the disruptive Covid pandemic?

On Our Approach to GAMEs
Updating cultural policy is hard and time consuming. Cutler's powerful approach to designing problem-solving GAMEs (Guidelines, Arena, Materials, Experience) has helped my team develop innovative ideas that rapidly adapt and expand existing support mechanisms for the "new normal."

Donna Walker-Kuhne
Founder,
Walker International Communications Group

MARKETING

My Challenge:
How do we build, engage, and sustain diverse communities when promoting projects and products?

On Our Approach to Building Teams
Cutler and his team have a distinctly dynamic approach to training and providing entrepreneurial experiences to multicultural participants. Doing so ensures that important assumptions get challenged, new perspectives are considered, and ultimate solutions are significantly richer.

Dr. Dilhani J. Uswatte
Principal,
Rocky Ridge Elementary

EDUCATION

My Challenge:
Develop a strategy to ignite long-term curiosity such that students truly become lifelong learners.

On Our Approach to Training Teams
This book made me realize that as a principal, I need to foster the right conditions for innovative thinking. It will not just happen magically. Efforts must be made to proactively train the team and create an energizing space where "WOW" thinking happens NOW.

John Simpkins
President & Chief
Executive Officer,
MDC

LEADERSHIP

My Challenge:
Envision an initiative that brings historically marginalized groups into the leadership circle of at least 10 companies.

On Chapter 1 & Defining Problems
Think big AND get to the point. Through the timeless wisdom of Mother Goose and beyond, this chapter offers practical, actionable advice on how to frame creative challenges, surface ideas from the team, and motivate change.

Ramone Dickerson
Executive Chef and
Co-Owner,
2 Fat 2 Fly

RESTAURANTS

My Challenge:
If we were 20 times bigger, how would our business model look?

On Chapter 2 & Innovation Conditions
Since reading this, my thinking has evolved regarding what it means to build a successful team. Considering which tasks are best suited for soloists, like-minded specialists, diverse communities, and even "non-puzzler participants" has created a COMPLETELY new level of clarity for my problem-solving approach!

Jeremy Leung
Associate Director,
Corporate Relations and
Sponsorships,
Carnegie Hall

PHILANTHROPY

My Challenge:
When pitching to new donors, how can we make a compelling case without creating information overload?

On Chapter 3 & Problem-Solving Tools
This chapter showed me how physical and virtual materials can transform problem solving with a team like mine. Strategic tools help convey an idea, inspire and galvanize stakeholders, and ultimately bring concepts to life. (At least, that's what I wrote on a newly acquired sticky note.)

Rosanna Stephens
Manager, Digital
Workplace Experience,
Adobe

TECHNOLOGY

My Challenge:
Design a connected digital work environment that fosters flexibility, well-being, collaboration, and productivity.

On Chapter 4 & Experience Design
As a tech leader focused on digital experiences, I find constraints crucial to creativity, like banks of a river allowing water to flow. This chapter gave me many ideas to help build new riverbanks so we can flow together in directions never imagined!

**Michelle
Logan-Owens,
DHA, RN**
Chief Operating Officer,
*McLeod Regional
Medical Center*

My Challenge:
Improve the patient and family experience by reducing the wait between procedure arrival and start time.

On Chapter 5 & Problem-Solving Lenses
The delivery of exceptional patient-centered care requires efficient and effective problem solving. The 5 lenses of innovation require teams to stay focused. They ensure that valuable inputs aren't overlooked, but are considered at the appropriate time. With the dynamics of the healthcare environment, I am grateful to have discovered this power tool!

Lou Kennedy
Chief Executive Officer,
*Nephron Pharmaceuticals
Corporation*

My Challenge:
How might we maintain a family-like small business culture while growing beyond our wildest expectations?

On Chapter 6 & Research Strategy
As we undertake new projects amid historic expansion, this chapter reminds me that my leadership team must ask many questions, listen carefully, and ensure no vital details go unnoticed. The most innovative companies glean a thorough understanding of critical challenges by carefully collecting accurate data, with an eye to the end goal.

Liela Shadmani
First Sergeant,
US Army

My Challenge:
Revamp professional military curriculum to focus on leadership experience and best practices.

On Chapter 7 & Creative Exploration
Designing better ways to cultivate honorable, physically fit, combat-ready Army teams requires creative visioning. Techniques that I learned from this chapter have helped my team question long-held assumptions and reimagine our approach in powerful ways.

Joe Zenas
Chief Executive Officer,
Thinkwell Group

My Challenge:
What if we visualized an exhilarating amusement park region based upon a popular video game franchise?

On Chapter 8 & Feedback
When designing creative experiences with my team, giving and receiving constructive feedback is essential. However, finding a delicate, direct balance can be challenging. The tools in this chapter provide a valuable, user-friendly foundation for improving this process and solutions that emerge. (How's that for a blue lens?)

Robert Harding
Senior Director of
Operations,
XPO Logistics

SUPPLY CHAIN

My Challenge:
Define a strategy to recruit, train, and retain drivers and dockworkers in a rapidly changing transportation job market.

On Chapter 9 & Making Choices
This chapter got me thinking about paralysis by analysis. In a company like mine, we need to nurture a fast-paced culture where teams successfully make and own decisive action. Try fast, fail fast, try again. Armed with these techniques, I choose to implement better protocols come time to decide.

Atiya Aftab
Co-Founder,
*Sisterhood of
Salaam Shalom*

SOCIAL JUSTICE

My Challenge:
How might we better facilitate meaningful, honest interfaith exchanges?

On Chapter 10 & Facilitating
My organization creates brave spaces where Muslim and Jewish women (who often never met before) develop empathic relationships and respect for "the other." Doing so requires master facilitation. Reading this, I realize the necessity of spending more time "training the trainers." Techniques in this step-by-step guide are immediately applicable and actionable.

Irma Muñoz
Founder/Executive
Director,
Mujeres de la Tierra

ENVIRONMENT

My Challenge:
Form a partnership that draws traditionally excluded communities of color to public beaches.

On Chapter 11 & Team Dynamics
This chapter immediately intrigued me because of its title. Collaborating with happy, positive people makes a project enjoyable and achievable. The focus on prickly personalities and champion collaboration transformed my thinking on team dynamics, including my own contribution style. *The GAME of Innovation* has become my manual for team-based work.

Clayton Mooney
Co-Founder & CEO,
Nebullam, Inc.

ENTREPRENEURSHIP

My Challenge:
Imagine an engaging new experience wrapped around our product for current/ future customers.

On Chapter 12 & Training Teams
"Shrink then explode" is a powerful framework for solving BIG problems. "Dreams first, then logistics" reminds me not to lose sight of what matters most. This chapter reignited my love for owning a niche. Now it's time to get to work . . . the GAME of work!

1 2 3 4 5 6 7 8 9 LWI 27 26 25 24 23 22

ISBN   978-1-264-25748-5   e-ISBN   978-1-264-25749-2
MHID   1-264-25748-1   e-MHID   1-264-25749-X

McGraw Hill books are available at special quantity discounts to use as premiums and sales promotions or for use in corporate training programs. To contact a representative, please visit the Contact Us pages at www.mhprofessional.com

McGraw Hill is committed to making our products accessible to all learners. To learn more about the available support and accommodations we offer, please contact us at accessibility@mheducation.com. We also participate in the Access Text Network (www.accesstext.org), and ATN members may submit requests through ATN.

THE GAME of INNOVATION

Contents

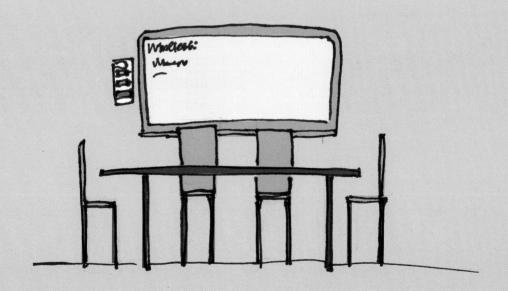

PART B: Color Your Perspective

PART C: **Playing to Win**

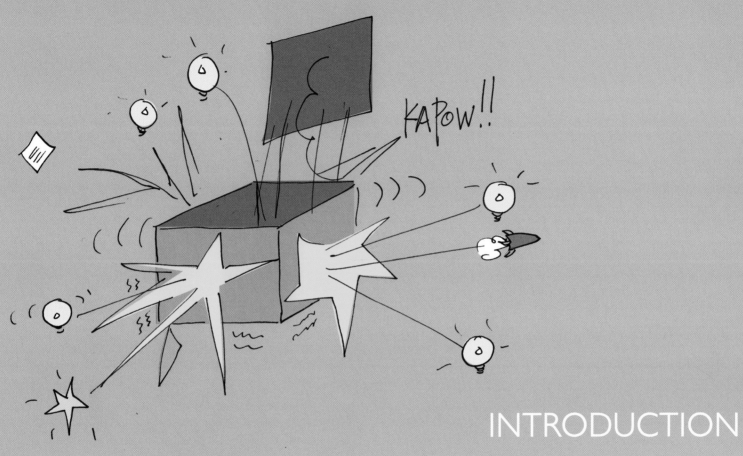

INTRODUCTION

GOT INNOVATION???

GOT INNOVATION???

It's almost cliché.

Leigh Durr maintains a position of prominence in a celebrated organization. She is good at what she does and widely respected.

Unfortunately, following many years of prosperity, the future looks precarious. Profits are down. New competitors have emerged. Fresh alternatives render their operational model antiquated.

Following months of denial and hand-wringing, Leigh recognizes an urgent need to address the elephant in the room. She convenes her community for an important conversation.

"We have so much to be proud of. Each of you has contributed significantly to our purpose-driven history. Sadly, the old way no longer works," Leigh conveys with a weak, empathetic smile. "Though change is always hard, we must reimagine the future.

INNOVATION is our only hope."

The team knows she is right.

But what that entails is anybody's guess.

Defining Innovation

Few buzzwords today are as pervasive as

INNOVATION.

Job descriptions stress the need for innovative leadership.

Organizations strive to promote an innovative culture.

Continuous innovation represents the best chance for sustainable business success.

Nonprofits seek innovative solutions to eradicate social ills like poverty and inequity.

Cities compete to attract the innovation sector.

Educators aim to nurture innovative thinkers.

Gig economy workers must design innovative career paths.

But what exactly does *innovation* mean?
Why is it vital to success?
And how effectively do you tap into its potential?

Here's my definition:

in-no-va-tion = *extraordinary problem solving*

CREATIVE CHALLENGES

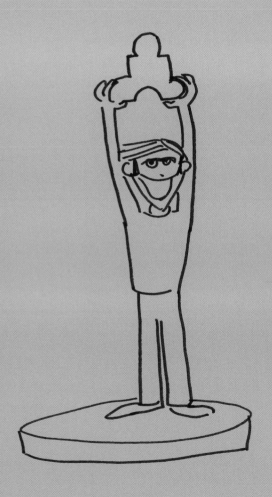

. . . confront essentially every LEADER

. . . and every TEAM

. . . from every DEPARTMENT

. . . of every ORGANIZATION

. . . at every LEVEL.

Our world evolves at an unprecedented pace, thanks to phenomena like disruptive technology, climate change, and globalization. New leadership, policies, business models, products, and tastes introduce obstacles and opportunities too significant to ignore.

There's a better way to do just about everything.
If you don't get there soon, you may be left behind.

CHANGE is the only guarantee.

No wonder innovation is in such demand!

Extraordinary problem solving is key to achieving excellence, efficiency, attention, demand, relevance, sustainability, harmony.

Many people mistakenly believe innovators are born, not made. It's as if the great heavens above opened for some mythological god to decree:

(And the rest of you uninspired folk? Go forth, chase the obvious, and be average.)

In truth, innovation can and must be cultivated.

Achievement requires adequate time, team, tools, techniques, tenacity . . . *and tons of practice.*

Extraordinary problem solving is part art, part science. It's a skill that improves with experience and an experience that requires skills.

My consulting firm, The Puzzler Company, features a team of artist-leaders known for innovating the field of innovation.

Our keynotes, workshops, and gamified problem-solving experiences empower business, education, arts, nonprofit, and government teams to crack the codes of creative success.

Engagements emphasize process and technique at least as much as getting to the solution. More important than conquering a particular issue is cultivating transferable skills and an aligned, entrepreneurial environment equipped to tackle change and challenge, whatever the future may hold.

Over the years, The Puzzler Company has designed, tweaked, and amplified an arsenal of tactics that help communities of all stripes conquer challenges, level up their team, and play to win.

The resulting methodology, unveiled in this book, will help you and your community thrive when playing *The GAME of Innovation.*

Why You Should Become a Champ

Not everyone aspires to the title of "innovation champion."

Many employees aren't paid to think. Or they have no interest in doing so. *Just follow directions.*

And then there are folks who reside in Euphoria and work in Utopia. Life is glorious—no need to tweak what already works!

Most of us, however, have no choice BUT to tackle important challenges. We are regularly called upon to discover the new, the noteworthy, the superior.

SUCCESS demands innovation.

If that describes your reality, master the sport of extraordinary problem solving. Such a distinction is particularly beneficial to:

Leaders	Team "captains" of all types and levels must motivate stakeholders to invent/adopt measures that propel aspirations.
Managers	These administrators are charged with coordinating projects, increasing productivity, and getting things done—complex challenges in themselves.
Instigators	Ironically, many appointed leaders have so many responsibilities, there is little time for actual leading. Change agents must emerge from within the ranks.
Collaborators	Problem-solving chops pay dividends for team members who confront creative dilemmas.
Entrepreneurs	Beyond inventing unique products or services, entrepreneurs must bring concepts to prominence by claiming market share.

Professionals	Many job titles inherently imply a problem-to-be-solved: educator, marketer, fundraiser. Established formulas may not suffice, making exploration necessary.
Underdogs	To improve fate, there is no option but to explore new strategies.
Returning Champs	Historic winners may have a tougher challenge. Already on top, there is little urgency to evolve. Yet, what got you *here* probably won't get you *there*.
Consultants	External voices are hired precisely because of their ability to diagnose weaknesses and propose uncommon solutions.
Trainers	Coaches across disciplines benefit when adding to their toolbox.
Aspirants	The sooner students, rising leaders, and other ambitious contributors develop innovation skills, the better off they—and the world—will be.

"We cannot solve our problems with the same level of thinking that created them."

—Albert Einstein, German physicist

Some Words of Warning

Warning

Most who advocate INNOVATION haven't seen it in action.

For a word tossed around as routinely as *innovation*, it is shocking how many people—including even artists, entrepreneurs, and CEOs—have not encountered it firsthand. Their experience more likely centers around the opposite: lectures, conferences, top-down mandates, standardized testing, coloring within the lines.

As a result, first-time participants in the types of activities described in this book often emerge with their minds pleasantly blown. The experience is wholly foreign, as if being teleported to another planet.

WARNING

2

Warning

Your WORLDVIEW may never again look the same.

Engaging with a true innovation process—how it looks, sounds, feels—changes people. Deeply held assumptions long taken for granted start to be questioned.

Suddenly, opportunities are everywhere, as well as fresh ways to get there.

Warning 3

Your TEAM may never again be the same.

When done well, team-based problem solving offers a deep, rich, addictive experience.

Beyond solving the challenge, it can amplify commitment, teach skills, emphasize values, build consensus, and elevate morale.

Previously risk-averse groups begin leaning into change rather than fleeing the scene. Collaboration becomes an anticipated, empowering adventure. Silos are abandoned. Ambition is enhanced.

Warning 4

Your MEETINGS may never again be the same.

Ah, the infamous, dreaded *meeting*. Renowned for passive information sharing and long-winded diatribes of questionable relevance, these "brain dumps" are widely considered unfortunate but necessary evils.

Why not transform your class/conference/board/department/company session into an exhilarating problem-solving experience?

Doing so can advance goals, increase productivity, and strengthen community. But beware that participants may soon lose patience for traditional, mind-numbing alternatives.

Warning 5

This is not an ANSWER key.

If you hope flipping to page 137 will reveal the elusive fix that's escaped your imagination for years, prepare to be disappointed. The point here is not to disclose *my* ingenuity. Rather, this book offers frameworks and tools that foster innovation. To yield dividends, however, the creative genius of you and your team must be engaged.

Warning 6

There is no magic FORMULA.

Innovation does not result from a cookie cutter process. Even Stanford University's brand of *design thinking*, which represents a powerful problem-solving approach, is not suited to every situation.

Consider each experience to be as unique as the challenge itself. The methodology unveiled here is specific and transferable, yet highly malleable. Rather than dogmatically employing rigid practices, apply what is meaningful in context.

How to "Play" This Book

The GAME of Innovation teaches strategies for discovering the remarkable. The secret?

Gamify challenges, level up your team, and play to win.

This book will help you:

Design powerhouse PROCESSES

Successfully tackle each PHASE

Maximize personal ABILITIES

Discover WOW innovation

Lead and manage TEAMS

Numerous stories demonstrate how principles apply to wide-ranging scenarios. While characters are fictional—we begin with inspiration from nursery rhymes (Chapter 1)—lessons are transferable. Consider how each can help conquer your challenge(s).

I recommend first reading *The GAME of Innovation* cover to cover. After an initial pass, treat it like a reference manual, returning to concepts as needed.

Far from a "one point book," these pages burst with strategy. But the most important lesson might be this:

Be intentional when tackling problems—and life.

The GAME of Innovation is organized as follows:

PREMISE: Problems, Pitfalls, & Play

Defining "problems," common obstacles to innovation, and a novel proposal.

PART A: Gamify Challenges (Chapters 1–4)

Build powerhouse problem-solving experiences with a flexible GAME approach.

PART B: Color Your Perspective (Chapters 5–9)

Streamline thinking when employing the five *lenses*, or perspectives, of innovation.

PART C: Playing to Win (Chapters 10–12)

Facilitate effectively, improve team dynamics, and arrive at the remarkable.

This book is a **visual guide**. Combining text and images throughout, it doesn't just talk about innovation. It *looks* like innovation.

Doing so serves several aims. I sincerely hope this graphic approach stimulates your imagination while enhancing enjoyment throughout the journey.

But there is also a pedagogical goal. Pictures are better than words alone at clarifying concepts and reinforcing details. This is but one reason so many problem-solving communities prioritize visual communication.

Contrary to popular belief:

Anybody and everybody can draw.

To that end, *The GAME of Innovation* serves as a tutorial. Conjure some courage and imitate what you see. Most doodles here combine simple shapes, lines, and scribbles. This is often true even when conveying complex ideas.

Consider which image types most powerfully suggest various messages. Next time you brainstorm or share a proposal, how might lessons learned be integrated?

Leigh Durr (introduced on page 6) understands that success demands nothing short of extraordinary problem solving.

For something this important, she and her team must

INNOVATE.

Why not turn it into a GAME?

START HERE

PROBLEMS, PITFALLS, & PLAY

Many teams fail to solve problems adequately,
let alone reach their innovation potential.
Here are common pitfalls, plus a bold proposal.

Why are problems so hard to solve?

PROBLEMS, PITFALLS, & PLAY

Let's face it.

You've got a whopper of a problem!

It's a puzzle that's presented itself where you work, live, volunteer, attend, visit, or otherwise contribute. Perhaps it's triggered by a large-scale societal ill, localized institutional goal, or pressing professional challenge. Whatever the specifics, you are responsible for delivering a powerhouse solution with real-world implications.

This is not the kind of problem resolved with an abacus, computer algorithm, or simple prescribed formula. There is no single "correct" answer, secured by rote knowledge and committed persistence alone.

Innovation is key.

Problem solving is often considered a soft skill. And there is indeed an art to cracking life's complex puzzles. No book can offer a guaranteed, universal formula. Each problem is special, requiring unique consideration and committed care.

But there are concrete strategies transferable to just about any challenge. Like great mathematicians and musicians, innovation champions have chops.

Problems are everywhere.

It's what you do with them that counts.

IT'S ALL PROBLEMS

Problems Are Opportunities

"Problem" is how I describe most tasks in life.

Any question or project is a problem of sorts, from the tragic to the mundane to the extraordinary. Branch openings, new hires, and meaningful initiatives are *exciting* problems. Digitizing the paper trail is a *logistical* problem. Differentiating your organization is a *creative* problem.

To-do lists are problem inventories.

"Problem" often carries negative connotations, describing unambiguously bad news. Many communities are concerned about their lack of diversity and inclusiveness. Poverty, illiteracy, and violent crime are heartbreaking crises that plague society. A company's new competitor may threaten to disrupt its dominance or future existence. These consequential issues deserve serious attention.

Yet the face of adversity can catalyze extraordinary achievement.

Individuals and organizations often discover their true calling in response to foreboding obstacles. A closed door leaves room for others to open . . . if you are brave enough to get out of the way and proceed with intention.

Whether starting points are positive or negative, the problems we pursue—as well as those that chase us mercilessly—define our unique existence. They shape our lives.

Let's face it. If your business is smaller, or bigger, or poorer, or newer, or less famous than the competition, those are tremendous problems.

Said another way, they are spectacular opportunities.

"A problem is a chance for you to do your best."

—Duke Ellington, American composer and bandleader

Problems Are Puzzles

Throughout this book, these terms are used interchangeably:

Problem —— **PUZZLE**
Problem Solver —— **PUZZLER**

Puzzle Type 1:
Follow the Directions

Like a recipe, Follow the Directions (FTDs) arrive with detailed instructions. Do as you're told to get a nice, predictable result.

The steps to success are predefined.

Franchise handbooks detail the "right" way to address every conceivable situation: flip the burger, dress in blue, charge this much. Organizations provide word-for-word scripts addressing common scenarios.

It's helpful to have an answer key!

FTDs are not necessarily easy. Some are inherently tricky, despite foolproof guidelines. The process becomes exasperating when instructions involve incoherent language or skipped essentials. At this point, your primary challenge becomes deciphering what the heck to do.

With persistence, however, such puzzles are almost always solvable. Standardized formulas help the less talented while hindering the gifted. Consider our recipe. For those who are clueless in the kitchen, this is a godsend. But for a Michelin star chef, it's the kiss of death. If you want magic, let them envision their own course.

FTDs are NOT puzzles of innovation.

Puzzle Type 2:
Get This Answer

"The World's Most Difficult Jigsaw Puzzle," manufactured by Paul Lamond Games, involves 529 double-sided pieces (though "it feels more like 4,000," according to Amazon). *There is no instruction manual,* only a picture on the box revealing the target design: a dense assembly of black and white Dalmatians.

Despite extreme complexity, some tricks can help (spoiler alert). Start with the frame and work inward. Several hints are embedded. For example, one dog wears a collar.

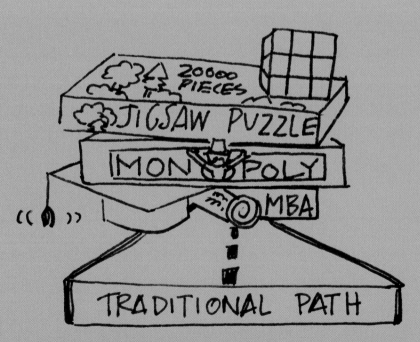

Like FTDs, many Get This Answer (GTA) assignments are delivered with desirable, predetermined solutions. Industry norms, best practices, and historic precedent suggest desirable outcomes.

The question becomes how to get there. No two attempts follow quite the same route. To win big, strategy is required.

GTA innovation explores unique paths to a well-defined endgame.

Beware of common GTA pitfalls:

Misleading **TARGETS**

Traditional solutions often contradict what matters most. Said another way, people focus on WHAT success looks like before evaluating WHY.

Misadvised **PRESSURES**

External forces like peer pressure, conventional wisdom, and societal trends attempt to impose priorities. Are those visions truly best for you?

Misguided **EXPECTATIONS**

In today's unpredictable world, "one-size-fits-all" solutions are rarely gratifying or amply rewarded.

Misplaced **FOCUS**

When consumed with "prepackaged" outcomes, meaningful opportunities that diverge from this route often go unrecognized.

Your challenge is not the same as your neighbor's. A more nuanced, personalized puzzle may be preferable.

A Puzzling Secret

Obvious solutions are often the least likely to pay off.

Picture the world as a high-rise. The goal—*success*—is located on the top floor. There is no elevator, only a narrow staircase.

Thousands of puzzlers pack themselves inside, chasing "normal" solutions to win the rat race. Some fall, others get trampled, several get stuck.

And every once in a while, a lucky new player makes it to the top.

You have a choice to make.

You can join the chaos, take the same stairs, face the same challenges. Or . . .

You can seek a different approach.

Maybe you crawl up the fire escape. Perhaps a friend's helicopter can make a rooftop drop, or you work out an agreement with the window washer.

Alternatively, maybe your version of success is located at a different address altogether.

Each new solution introduces risk. However, isn't there also peril in the heavily trafficked journey? Most travelers take these steps without considering alternatives. There's a sad irony:

The staircase is often the most difficult route.

"If you are always trying to be normal,
you will never know how amazing you can be."

—Maya Angelou, American poet, memoirist, and civil rights activist

Puzzle Type 3:
Paint Your Own

When an artist meets a canvas, the realm of possibility is truly infinite. With the full permission, responsibility, and opportunity to Paint Your Own (PYO), puzzlers choose their dyes, brushes, colors, textures, techniques, and approach. No two depictions are quite the same.

PYOs are the most common type of puzzle, and often the most meaningful. After all, you are the artist assigned to your own life.

Perhaps you want to launch a product, stand out from competition, or make more money. Maybe it's a social challenge like increasing literacy or minimizing pollution. Or it could be an issue like institutional culture, whether employee turnover is high or community morale low.

All of these present an opportunity—and mandate—to discover fantastically personal solutions.

PYO innovation showcases your own unique vision.

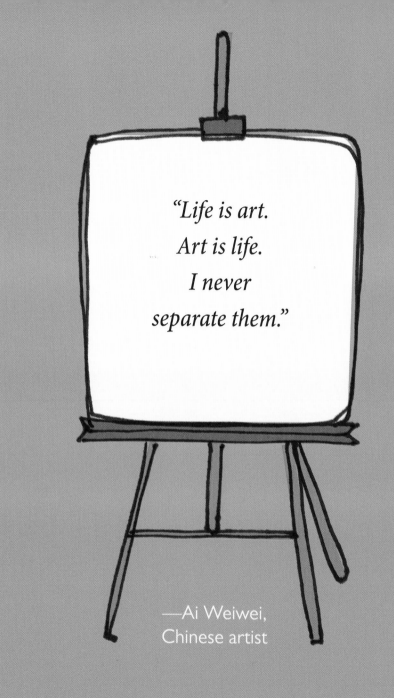

*"Life is art.
Art is life.
I never
separate them."*

—Ai Weiwei,
Chinese artist

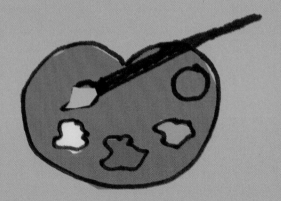

PYOs sometimes masquerade as FTDs or GTAs, but don't be fooled.

Important challenges rarely beckon prescribed formulas.

To be clear, PYOs don't imply that *everything* is possible.

Painters typically begin with a "blank" canvas. Yet even this object imposes real constraints. Perhaps it is 24" × 36" and made of linen. Though any approach or image type may be fair game, size and material play an outsized role in shaping the ultimate vision.

Most puzzlers face a BIG challenge. Rather than starting from scratch, the background is prescribed. To succeed, their team must paint atop an institution's culture, history, inefficiencies, proud traditions, systemic ugliness.

It's as if the canvas for problem solvers were another, pre-existing piece of art. Suppose you were given Leonardo Da Vinci's *Mona Lisa* or Edvard Munch's *The Scream*, and asked to reenvision a fresh, meaningful creation. What a tremendous challenge and responsibility!

Many people wish away the limitations of work and reality. They use them as excuses for not changing, rather than clues for progress.

But innovation champions take another approach. As we will see, they understand a powerful principle:

Constraints are essential for invention.

Problems Are (Almost Always) Solvable

Not every problem can be unscrambled. Some are truly hopeless. No amount of money, resources, or brainpower can crack the code. But in the vast majority of cases, success is achievable.

Almost every puzzle in work and life can be solved.

With enough commitment, creativity, and resolve, demons can be exorcized. Treasure can be seized. Particularly when you start with "How can we win?" rather than "Is this possible?"

The news gets better. Puzzling isn't just about flukes of nature and slim margins of serendipity.

There are a thousand solutions to most puzzles.

Of course, not all are equivalent. They vary wildly in design and impact, falling along a spectrum. Many are acceptable, several good, and a few superb.

If what you do isn't working, no matter how hard you push, try something else. The potential to innovate is vast.

12
Puzzling Pitfalls

Let's face it.

You've got a whopper of a problem!

No, not that problem. The puzzle imagined on page 18 still demands attention. But that's not the reference here.

This problem is about *process*. It's about *strategy*. And it's about *team*.

Even diehard puzzlers struggle to innovate remarkable—or adequate—solutions. Their efforts end in stalemate, paralysis, downgraded aspirations, or outright desertion.

Solutions to the following pitfalls are addressed in corresponding chapters.

Pitfall **Faulty Framing**

There are many reasons individuals and organizations fail to acknowledge, let alone tackle, the most significant problems they face. Beware of urgent, less important issues that divert energy, imagination, and action from what matters most.

While problem solving, too many puzzlers dive in without clearly defined parameters.

Success is a vague, fuzzy poof, with no tangible guideposts. Limits are too restrictive or nonexistent. As a result, the wheels turn mightily, but journeyers short-circuit while spinning in circles.

Addressed: Chapter 1

Inadequate Conditions

Pitfall **2**

Problem-solving efforts can be doomed before they begin.

A team may be inadequate. The mix of perspectives is insufficient, lacking expertise, qualifications, permission, work ethic, or diversity of worldviews.

In a world of busyness and over-commitment, important puzzles are frequently deprived of the time they deserve. Yet others suffer the opposite fate, with no urgency in sight.

Some venues just aren't conducive to collaboration or feel antithetical to creativity.

Addressed: Chapter 2

Pitfall 3 — Mismatched Tools

There's a reason innovators stockpile Post-its, flip charts, Sharpies, dice, yarn, LEGOs. *Materials matter.*

The wrong tool for a given task slows action and compromises results. Promising proposals get buried, too difficult to sort or locate. Critical details are camouflaged thanks to small fonts, bland colors, and too many words. Ineffective mechanisms discourage precise tactical planning.

Addressed: Chapter 3

Pitfall 4 — Ineffective Processes

Brilliant solutions are unlikely to magically appear. Reaching a desirable destination requires intentionality when planning the journey. While each stop allows ample room for exploration, the sequence and content of each phase is of paramount importance.

Yet many teams attempt to solve problems with no apparent process beyond, "Here's the issue. What should we do?" Jumping in without a clear, cohesive strategy is flirting with failure.

Addressed: Chapter 4

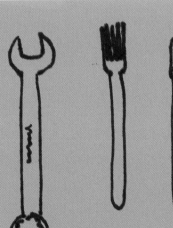
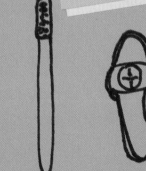

Pitfall

5 Alignment Issues

Even groups that genuinely get along often feel like they're fighting at every step. As one person examines the past, someone else brainstorms, while another critiques. A well-intentioned leader works to build consensus behind one idea—*any idea*—while teammates expand the roster of possibility.

As a result, conversation never builds momentum. Perspectives don't gel. The team moves at a sloth-like pace, or gets stuck altogether. *So much is said, yet so little gets done.*

Addressed: Chapter 5

Pitfall

6 Incorrect Assumptions

Faulty, untested assumptions often mask the real problem. Resources are deemed off limits before anyone investigates. The wrong customer, or deadline, or value proposition is presupposed sacrosanct.

In most cases, we don't even understand these things are assumptions. With insufficient research, we naïvely believe *that's just the way it is; that's how it always will be.*

Addressed: Chapter 6

Pitfall 7

Lack of Creativity

Not everyone feels creative. Some puzzlers believe they simply weren't wired that way. Unable to imagine alternatives to the status quo, they bow out.

Others believe the exact opposite. *They are the change*, at least in their own minds. So please understand the reluctance to tinker further.

And then there's a third group, perhaps the largest. Though sincerely committed to the notion of exploration, they lack a toolkit for catapulting into uncharted terrain.

Addressed: Chapter 7

Pitfall 8

Poor Feedback

Improvement requires honest feedback. Yet some groups tiptoe on eggshells. Whether terrified to rock the boat or lacking analytical depth, shallow analysis ensures that no concept is properly vetted.

Others are so negative, they zap enthusiasm. No detail is too small to be torn to shreds. Constant critique guarantees that meaningful progress cannot be made. Even when perpetuated by just a few voices, puzzlers get caught in this rabbit hole.

Addressed: Chapter 8

Pitfall 9

Inability to Decide

Rather than committing to one thing at the expense of many others, solutions are hoarded.

Can't we do them all?

Making hard decisions in a world ripe with opportunity is tough for the ambitious. That challenge amplifies when competing agendas must reach consensus.

Addressed: Chapter 9

Weak Leadership

Someone must shape the conversation, excite the tribe, keep trains running, and focus genius.

Yet facilitators routinely make rookie mistakes. They contribute too much, listen too little, provide vague instructions. In an instant, the schedule or focus can swerve off track.

Without the right kind of guidance, your game is surely lost.

Addressed: Chapter 10

10   Pitfall

Unhappy Teams

Pitfall

Unclear expectations, long-winded answers, unequal participation, and annoying distractions slow momentum while derailing progress. Prickly personalities torpedo morale as puzzlers backstab, cling to the status quo, and fight for personal ambitions over organizational priorities.

Puzzling is demanding, both mentally and physically. The mood can turn south.

Addressed: Chapter 11

Anemic Solutions

Despite sincere intentions and a well-planned process, conclusions frequently underwhelm. Fear or insecurity triggers a retreat to safety.

A lack of skills, the wrong puzzlers, or turf wars obstruct the remarkable.

Yes, a solution emerges. But it's far from a WOW.

Addressed: Chapter12

Pitfall   12

One Final Pitfall

Suppose you're the new boss, community director, head honcho. As you look around, one point becomes clear.

This place has problems.

Luckily, you see opportunity where others find roadblocks. After tweaking, shuffling, and reorganizing, things are finally headed in the right direction thanks to your astute wisdom!

Until one day, you get reprimanded. Or fired. Or face a mutiny. *What happened?*

It's possible your ideas stink. No kingpin has all the answers. But I'd place money on another culprit.

The notion of a fresh face shaking things up is almost always met with resistance. The merits of your vision or positive personal intent are deemed irrelevant. People dig in and push back.

Here's some advice for leaders, particularly within historically rooted organizations. It may sound counterintuitive:

Don't be the idea person.

That's not the gig!

What leaders can and should do is:

- Set the narrative.
- Ask big questions.
- Shape the culture.
- Design meaningful experiences.

Meticulously create the puzzle, while empowering stakeholders to become innovation champions.

Turn it into a GAME.

Beyond expanding the pool of wisdom, such an approach is exponentially more likely to generate enthusiasm. Tapping into a community's collective genius builds buy-in and pays dividends, big time.

The **GAME** of Innovation

What if you approached important challenges as if they were games of profound consequence? Why not treat them with the discipline, tactics, and resolve of a skilled Olympian? Which problem will you confront? Who forms the team? What will they do? How is victory defined?

Problem solving isn't just about SOLUTIONS.

Innovation champions begin by building a great process. Their GAMEs are governed by clear rules that all sides must accept to commence play. *No deviation permitted.*

Implying more than an activity type, GAME describes a strategically designed structure.

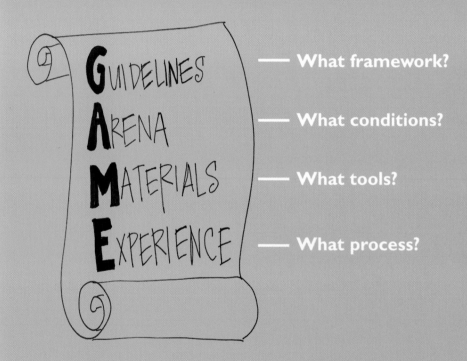

— **What framework?**

— **What conditions?**

— **What tools?**

— **What process?**

I refer to any well-planned problem-solving experience as a GAME, whether or not it involves dice, cards, or other "game-y" features.

While playful elements offer benefits, this book helps teams of all stripes tackle even the most serious creative problems.

Why play GAMEs with your future?

Innovation is far from trivial pursuits. If the issue truly matters, treat it like a battle of epic proportions. Success is exponentially more likely with well-designed experiences. Good GAMEs bring:

Purpose

Communities unify behind collective aspirations.

Accountability

Unambiguous guidelines provide metrics for measuring success.

Strategy

Intentional, tactical maneuvering is compulsory.

Creativity

Exploration is welcome, required, and embedded.

Motivation

Competition inspires puzzlers to push harder.

Fun

GAMEs can be hard, but great experiences inspire!

On second thought, why wouldn't you?

■ Culture is a game.
Work is a game.
Money is a game.
Adversity is a game.
Success is a game.

If it truly matters,
play to WIN . . .

PART A
GAMIFY CHALLENGES

Well before exploring solutions,
design your innovation **GAME**.

GAMIFY CHALLENGES

Part A OVERVIEW

When confronting creative challenges, people too often jump impatiently to answers. This approach is unlikely to work. Innovation rarely erupts in a flash. True, there may be bursts of sudden inspiration, but with few exceptions:

Extraordinary solutions result from carefully architected PROCESSES.

Part A of this book focuses exclusively on designing "innovation GAMEs." Though scenarios are supplied throughout to contextualize, the problems themselves are not solved at this point, for good reason. Effective problem solving begins by building deeply meaningful experiences, rather than considering results. That's up to your puzzlers, during play. (Sample solutions appear beginning in Part B.)

A separate chapter is devoted to each GAME element (**G**uidelines, **A**rena, **M**aterials, **E**xperience).

Chapter 1

Establishing a framework for innovation, **GUIDELINES** pinpoint a clearly defined problem (**C**hallenge), nonnegotiables (**C**onstraints), and success metrics (**C**riteria).

Chapter 2

Addressing the conditions you have to work with, an **ARENA** defines your mix of problem solvers (**P**uzzlers), time frame (**P**eriod), and physical/virtual environment (**P**lace).

Chapter 3

MATERIALS, the tools of innovation, include a variety of supplies (**G**atherables), specialty game items (**G**ear), and mapping canvases (**G**ameboards).

Chapter 4

When building an **EXPERIENCE,** determine the GAME type (**S**orts) and sequence of activities (**S**tructure). This chapter concludes with several examples (**S**amples).

CHAPTER I

GUIDELINES

Establishing a framework for innovation, GUIDELINES pinpoint a clearly defined problem (**C**hallenge), nonnegotiables (**C**onstraints), and success metrics (**C**riteria).

What framework?

GUIDELINES

Winning big in work and life requires more than masterful solving. The first test?

Play the right GAME.

The puzzles you embrace and how they define success impact critical resources like energy, time, and money. Begin your quest by strategically framing important problems in meaningful ways.

Innovation champions build clear, concise *Guidelines* that articulate three top-level parameters (**C**hallenge, **C**onstraints, **C**riteria). This framework plays an outsized role in shaping the process and ultimate outcome. Altering even a few words can dramatically shift the narrative.

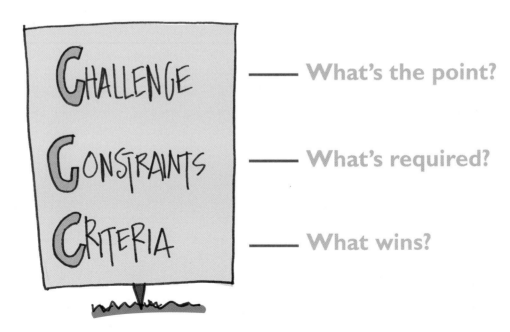

Challenge ——— **What's the point?**

Constraints ——— **What's required?**

Criteria ——— **What wins?**

Nursery rhymes offer a playful opportunity to consider problems from a nonthreatening perspective. We begin with several such examples before pivoting to real-world challenges later in this chapter.

> *Little Miss Muffet, sat on a tuffet,*
> *Eating her curds and whey;*
> *Along came a spider, who sat down beside her,*
> *And frightened Miss Muffet away.*

Little Miss Muffet has a big "wicked" problem. As she sits on a weatherproof tuffet in a peaceful park, a monstrous, hideous, wretched eight legged beast ruins everything!

Gripped by terror, Muffet flees. Dropping lunch on the ground, she sprains an ankle and is rushed to the hospital.

Recognizing the need to take action, Mother Goose organizes an innovation GAME. But which problem should be tackled? Eradicate bugs? Restore calm? Eliminate arachnophobia? Or should liabilities become assets, converting land into an insect park?

With careful consideration, she establishes *Guidelines*.

 CHALLENGE

Minimize spider invasions while maintaining ecological balance.

CONSTRAINTS

1. Must preserve natural order
2. May not contaminate human food items
3. Must be implementable within one year

CRITERIA

1. Visible elements are aesthetically pleasing
2. Deter other pests as well
3. Noteworthy solution increases park traffic
4. Replicable model adopted by neighboring communities

CHALLENGE

What's the point?

The previous chapter opened with the declaration, "You've got a whopper of a problem!" But face it—that's just part of the story. Challenges bombard us from every direction.

Life rarely allows the luxury of a single dilemma.

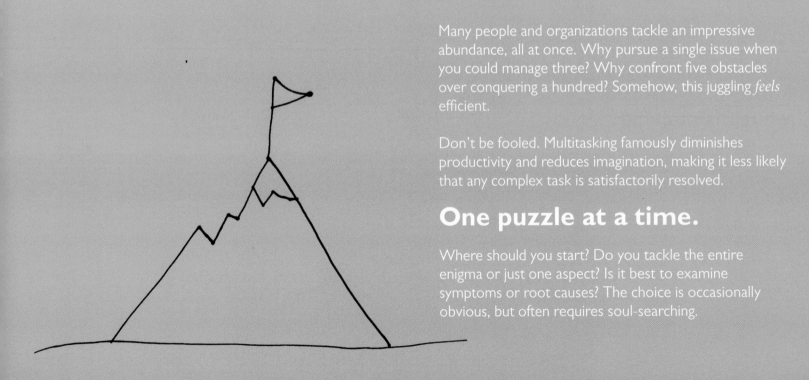

Many people and organizations tackle an impressive abundance, all at once. Why pursue a single issue when you could manage three? Why confront five obstacles over conquering a hundred? Somehow, this juggling *feels* efficient.

Don't be fooled. Multitasking famously diminishes productivity and reduces imagination, making it less likely that any complex task is satisfactorily resolved.

One puzzle at a time.

Where should you start? Do you tackle the entire enigma or just one aspect? Is it best to examine symptoms or root causes? The choice is occasionally obvious, but often requires soul-searching.

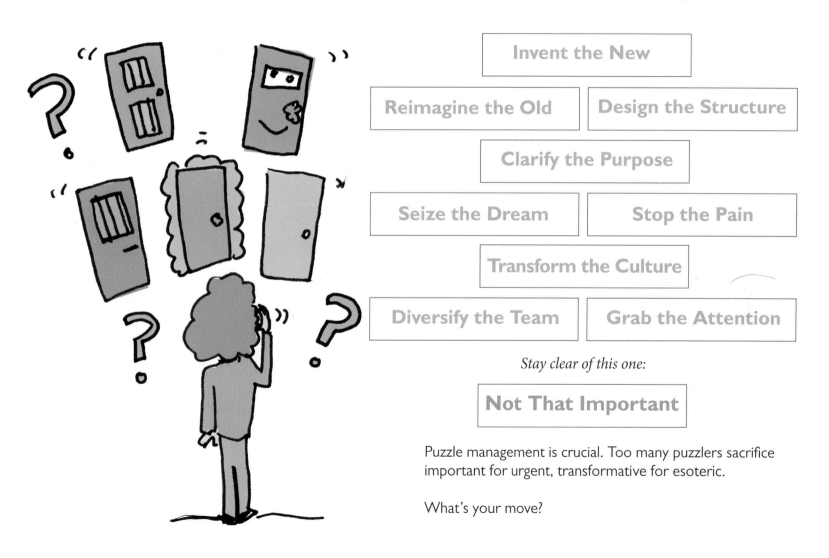

Choose Your Puzzle

The proverbial bookshelf in the playroom of life holds an infinite amount of challenges. While details are unique to each, underlying themes are widespread.

Invent the New

Reimagine the Old   Design the Structure

Clarify the Purpose

Seize the Dream   Stop the Pain

Transform the Culture

Diversify the Team   Grab the Attention

Stay clear of this one:

Not That Important

Puzzle management is crucial. Too many puzzlers sacrifice important for urgent, transformative for esoteric.

What's your move?

Prioritize Puzzles That Matter Most

Consider three puzzles. All are meaningful. But too often, the less important dominates.

ANNOYANCES

peripheral issues

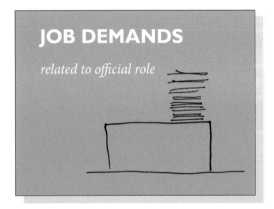

JOB DEMANDS

related to official role

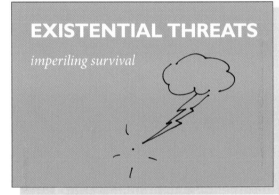

EXISTENTIAL THREATS

imperiling survival

Suppose there's a shortage of office parking. How can anything get done if folks can't stow their Chevies? Catapulted to priority status, your team starts puzzling. Miraculously, a solution emerges: "Request spaces in another lot, a block away." Everyone leaves validated. Parking for all! Problem solved!

From one perspective, this is a story of triumph. The new reality boosts morale. It feels liberating to get something accomplished!

But parking has nothing to do with the mission of this organization. It's a mere *annoyance* that distracts from important job demands . . .

Most conscientious workers believe their *job* is to do their job well. Puzzles are chosen accordingly. The actor rehearses with diligence; the manager tends to customer service. Without significant focus on such demands, there would be chaos, mayhem, total lack of coherence.

Yet this is where individuals, organizations, or even full industries sometimes die. So absorbed with the problem of the day—what we're supposed to do—there's no bandwidth left to address the distant tsunami of disruption, rising in strength. Until this *existential threat* suddenly hits, and BAM!

Game over.

Seek Puzzles That Interlock

We are often pulled in a hundred directions. Though efforts are meaningful in isolation,

Rival forces dilute the composite impact.

Multiple initiatives advance competing— even opposing—goals. Project A diminishes the potency of Project B, and vice versa. Work and family become adversaries to be "balanced," with progress on one side diminishing quality on the other.

In organizations, a culture of silos emerges. When asked, "What's the most important unique value your organization offers?" there are as many distinct answers as stakeholders. Fully absorbed with personal responsibilities and biases, tunnel vision fails to connect efforts to that of colleagues or institutional priorities.

Yet extraordinary success rarely results from a single solved puzzle, or even a bundle. The trick is compiling multiple highly connected wins, each pushing closer to an audacious, large-scale ambition. Small victories unlock bigger ones, but only when they fit together.

Suppose a small podcast company hopes to grow its bottom line. At first, they plan to launch shows on a range of compelling topics. With further consideration, they realize each broadcast would compete with others, requiring a distinct audience, marketing, connections, and so on. Instead, they opt to go narrow but deep, building an ever-expanding platform within a *single* focus, complete with merchandising, programming, and the full force of their energy.

Mind you, in this example, the same quantity of projects gets pursued. But a less fragmented, more cohesive, consolidated approach pays dividends.

Synergy beats disunity.

Carefully Diagnose the Puzzle

The object of the GAME is to confront a clearly defined challenge. Be sure you identify the right one.

> *Humpty Dumpty sat on a wall,*
> *Humpty Dumpty had a great fall,*
> *All the king's horses and all the king's men,*
> *Couldn't put Humpty together again.*

 CHALLENGE: How might we prevent future eggs from cracking upon impact?

You're likely familiar with the tragic demise of Earth's most famous egg, Humpty Dumpty. After plummeting from a precarious position, his shell shatters. Despite valiant attempts by top kingdom talent, Humpty is a lost cause. He simply can't be put back together again.

Mother Goose Elementary School is challenged to confront this dilemma. To minimize collision damage, student teams prototype contraptions incorporating every conceivable substance: egg cartons, mattresses, trampolines, bird nests, Jell-O ramps, masking tape mountains, cotton ball cocoons.

But one group isn't convinced. "What if we're solving the wrong problem?" they postulate. "How might we prevent future falls altogether?"

Problem diagnosis requires savvy strategy.

"We fail more often because we solve the wrong problem than because we get the wrong solution to the right problem."

—Russell L. Ackoff,
American organizational theorist

Narrow Your Focus

"Cure world hunger" is a noble aspiration. But even the biggest brains will fail. Unrealistically broad puzzles doom efforts before they begin.

When defining a GAME's scope, consider the hand you've been dealt: problem complexity, how long you have, capacity of puzzlers. When you can't solve it all, zoom in. Limit focus to part of the problem, known as a *Sector Solution*.

A SECTOR SOLUTION
addresses part of the problem

*Jack and Jill went up the hill,
to fetch a pail of water.
Jack fell down and broke his crown,
And Jill came tumbling after.*

★ **CHALLENGE: Improve our water retrieval system.**

Well before the age of plumbing, Jack and Jill were infamously tasked with collecting water from a well, high upon a hill. Unfortunately, they took a nasty tumble, resulting in concussions and a temporary drinking drought.

Mother Goose recognizes this problem is too complex for an upcoming 1½-hour council meeting. To isolate the best sector solution, she considers two questions:

1. What can reasonably be accomplished during a short 90-minute window?

2. Which micro-challenge will move us forward while motivating the community?

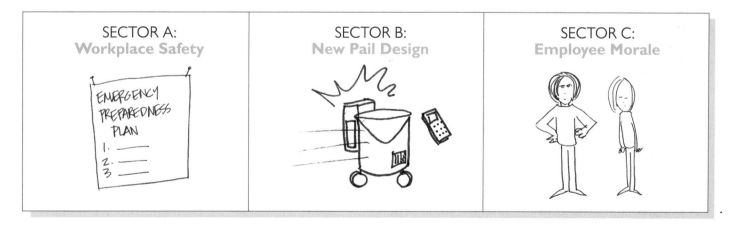

While all will eventually receive attention, she opts for "A," formulating a stringent set of safety regulations.

Puzzler Poetics

Craft *challenge statements* with the commitment of a poet, using succinct, comprehensible language.

Every word matters.

Question Statements

Question statements present open-ended inquiries. "How might we?" "What if?" and "If . . . what/how?" structures are particularly provocative.

- HOW MIGHT WE create a more diverse and inclusive environment?
- WHAT IF we "fired" our worst clients?
- IF we stopped meeting in person, WHAT would we do?
- IF we move across town, HOW might our business model change?

Action Statements

Action statements marry *action verbs* (amplify, design, reimagine, disrupt, etc.) with a premise.

- DESIGN an initiative that improves morale.
- BUILD an entrepreneurial venture.
- REIMAGINE our website.
- BOOST earnings.

"The difference between the right word and the almost right word is the difference between lightning and a lightning bug."

—Mark Twain, American writer and entrepreneur

Old to New

Challenge statements can underscore a problematic state.

- Update our business model, ORIGINALLY IMPLEMENTED in 1967.
- Transform our WORN, TIRED BUILDING into the most spectacular venue in town.
- Transition from my UNINSPIRING DAY JOB into a purpose-driven career.

Top Goal

Though success metrics are generally listed as Criteria, Challenge statements can embed one top-level priority.

- Restructure our staff so 3 MEMBERS FOCUS ON FUNDRAISING.
- Organize an event so unique it gets FEATURED IN NATIONAL MEDIA.
- How might an after school program reduce juvenile detention BY 20 PERCENT.

Consider a few final challenge statements from nursery rhymes. (If you aren't familiar, search online for the original poems.)

LONDON BRIDGE
CHALLENGE: Design an impenetrable overpass.

HICKORY DICKORY DOCK
CHALLENGE: Exterminate those pesky rodents.

OLD WOMAN WHO LIVED IN A SHOE
CHALLENGE: How might we systematize childcare, transforming replicable strategies into a franchisable, profit-generating venture?

CONSTRAINTS/CRITERIA
What's required? What wins?

A clearly defined *Challenge* statement is only the first requirement when building Guidelines. It is also necessary to identify concrete *Constraints* and *Criteria*.

Constraints	Criteria
Every GAME should present *nonnegotiables* that cannot be challenged. Include only what is necessary, disclosing all up-front. Otherwise, puzzlers may shape thoughtful solutions, only to learn that time was wasted wading in forbidden territory.	Where Constraints define the floor, Criteria look to the sky. Most often, they define success.
Some creatives argue against such limiters. "Do we really need Constraints? Can't we allow imaginations to run wild, like spider monkeys in the Amazon?" Though this sentiment is admirable, the request is misguided.	**To win, these standards must be met or exceeded.**
Restrictions are vital.	Some GAMEs take a different approach. The proverbial finish line is reached when projects achieve all Constraints. In this case, Criteria serve as bonuses, triggering extra credit.
They provide a starting point to push against or build around, while preventing problem-solving anarchy. Well-crafted Constraints force puzzlers to think differently, banning the safety of status quo or Captain Obvious.	Regardless of method, the trick is to ignite imagination and ambition *without* prescribing solutions.

Every point listed in a GAME's Guidelines, from C to shining C (**C**hallenge, **C**onstraints, **C**riteria), should focus energy, helping puzzlers make informed, strategic decisions.

Constraints and Criteria should be listed in priority order.

Ranked objectives further clarify what matters most. They provide guidance during play when one goal must come at the expense of another. Move from most to least important.

Sometimes there's debate: Is it a Constraint or Criterion? That depends how you frame the GAME. Note how even the same words have different implications in the final example that follows.

Constraints are requisite. Criteria are aspirational.

Constraints (What's required?)	Criteria (What wins?)
Audience: 150 high school seniors Attendance is compulsory, so make it relevant.	**Audience: 230 Latinx professionals** We'd love to attract this group.
Maximum budget = $10,000 We may not spend a penny more.	**Minimum earnings = $25,000** We hope to generate at least this much.
Packaged in a single box You may not use two.	**Packaged in a single box** Best-case scenario.

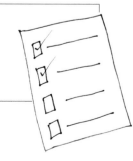

"Short Lists"
Identify Top Priorities

There are two general approaches when determining the quantity of Criteria and Constraints: short lists and long lists.

Most common are short lists, clarifying 2–5 top-level considerations.

★ CHALLENGE: Allocate resources to maximize community impact.

Harmony Township is delighted to receive a sizable grant for renovating their library. Unfortunately, the amount is half of what they asked for, meaning tough choices must be made.

Before meeting with their planning committee, project manager Kat A. Logger spends a good deal of time considering Guidelines. To determine success Criteria, she uses an approach called *Those Three Things.*

The object is identifying the trio of aspirations—not two, not four, exactly three—that matter most. She establishes the following ranked list:

Criteria

1. Innovative technology wing
2. Interactive children's area
3. Career education center

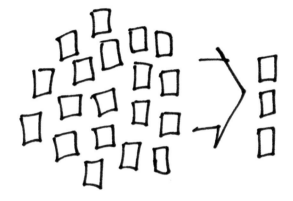

Formulating this list was excruciating. The most difficult aspect? Saying goodbye to many good possibilities: auditorium modernization, modular furniture, adding a cafeteria.

But clarity is liberating. These priorities become essential when mapping the future. And reflecting on them underscores two crucial points.

**What is most important.
And what is not.**

"Long Lists" Suggest Ambitions

While excessive Constraints are overbearing and not usually recommended, long lists of 10–20+ entries offer an intriguing approach to Criteria.

The goal:

Incorporate as many targets as possible.

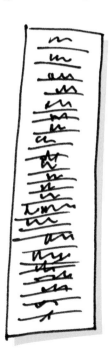

 **CHALLENGE:**

Organize the best Fall Fest to date.

Val Inteer is on the board of a homeowners' association. Part of her role involves orchestrating a 20th anniversary fundraising event to support community priorities.

Before planning begins, she identifies a prioritized long list of desirable Criteria. Note the combination of outcomes and features (page 54), fuzzy and concrete (page 56) goals.

1. Generate $5,000 profit
2. Safe environment
3. Fun activities for young kids
4. Fun activities for older siblings
5. Fun activities for parents
6. 35–50 volunteers
7. Strengthen community relationships
8. 30+ unique games
9. 8+ new games introduced
10. Playground integrated
11. Some homes integrated
12. Bouncy house
13. Local art featured
14. Raffle
15. Dunking booth
16. 75%+ neighborhood engaged
17. Fun prizes
18. Variety of food options

Eighteen is a lot of objectives. Val understands that not all are likely to come to fruition. But this inventory proves invaluable to the planning committee, who are challenged to realize "at least 13."

Outcomes vs. Features

Outcomes are conceptual, describing desired results. Consider whether to position each as a minimal requirement (Constraint) or optimal ideal (Criteria).

Outcomes

Beautiful design
Safety
Going viral

Features pinpoint specific aspects/attributes. As a rule, minimize the number of features listed as Criteria, at least on short lists. Pragmatic rather than aspirational, they tie hands, suggesting solutions before play begins. If a feature is truly requisite, include it as a Constraint.

Features

Dimensions	The office must remain 16 feet long, 22 feet wide, 10 feet high.
Time	The event is March 16.
Location	The venue must be within area code X.
Specs	The merry-go-round must include zebras and baboons.
Services	Our company performs lawn care and snow removal.
Elements	The show must include a 15-minute speech by the mayor.
Audience	Attendees will be senior citizens from Retirement Community Y.
Off limits	We cannot close the street to vehicle traffic.

CHALLENGE: Design a stylish reversible purse.

Recognizing the popularity of multifunction items, luggage designer Bay Gidge gives her product team this exciting assignment.

When building prioritized Guidelines, Bay is careful not to overprescribe. For example, there is no mention of materials or costs. Focused almost exclusively on outcomes, the team is granted creative control.

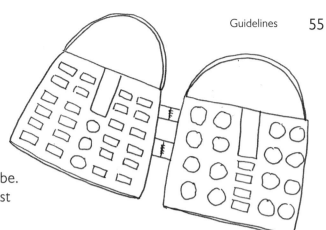

Constraints	
1. Dressy on one side, sporty on the other	Feature
2. Minimum dimensions: 12" W × 8" H × 6" D	Feature
3. Durable and high quality	Outcome

Criteria	
1. Eye popping	Outcome
2. Intuitive reversal process	Outcome
3. Ample storage space	Outcome
4. Incorporates suede trim	Feature
5. Wins a major design award	Outcome

Quantify When Possible

Concrete, measurable Guidelines are more easily assessed than fuzzy ones. The secret is including a number.

Fuzzy	Concrete
Packages delivered quickly	Packages delivered within **12** hours
Earn as much as possible!	Earn **$125,000** per quarter
Increase social media presence	Secure **18,000** social media followers
Read more	Read **3** books per month

Weigh the Psychology of Money

Few individuals or organizations have limitless resources. As a result, they may be tempted to impose maximum budgets when seeking innovation. However, I often recommend against financial constraints, at least early on. Start with the dream. Make it feasible later. If a remarkable idea requires more than is available, perhaps you can:

1. Scale things down to viability
2. Implement just the strongest elements
3. Identify new funding mechanisms

Overemphasis on fiscal practicality kills creativity.

Too many puzzlers mistakenly believe throwing cash at any problem is the obvious panacea. "We lack customers and interest; let's increase the advertising budget!" Conversely, insufficient funding becomes the scapegoat for countless obstacles.

Money will not solve all your problems.

That said, consider how exaggerated fiscal Guidelines might ignite creativity. One strategy involves cutting the allocation significantly. "Since we've historically failed with $10,000 . . . what if we had just three grand?" There is no choice but to explore *guerilla tactics* (low budget, high creativity).

The opposite also intrigues. Requiring a minimum budget of one million dollars for a traditional 10-dollar trinket pushes past small thinking, elevating ambitious lines of attack.

Extreme Guidelines catalyze radical solutioning.

 ## Deadlines Add a Taste of Reality

Time constraints force puzzlers to be grounded without sacrificing creativity in the name of fiscal pragmatism. Perhaps proposals must be implementable within a year or another predetermined period.

 ## CHALLENGE: Transform our lobby into a welcoming space.

Ed Mini-Strater insists on giving his workplace a makeover. While open to the exotic, he insists that this transformation doesn't drag on endlessly. A Constraint states that all work must be completed within three months.

Mandate Innovation!

It's a common story. A group of puzzlers commit to reinventing the world. Yet in the end, they retreat. Proposals seem oddly familiar, offering little more than surface tweaks and incremental change.

Why not bake innovation directly into the GAME?

 CHALLENGE: **How might we reimagine what we do and how we do it?**

Twenty years ago, First Tradition Bank thrived. Recently, they've bled clients. Unfortunately, past efforts to do things differently have triggered fierce opposition from employees clinging to the status quo.

The new CEO X. Perry Mint recognizes that staff will revolt if he imposes a change vision. Instead, they are brought into the process through a GAME. While no solutions are imposed, the following conditions are set.

Constraints

1. 20% of your proposal must be INNOVATIVE

2. 20% of your proposal must be TRADITIONAL

3. YOU DECIDE what to do with the remaining 60%

"The more constraints one imposes, the more one frees one's self."

—Igor Stravinsky, Russian composer

Of course, *innovation* and *tradition* are just words. So Perry defines several gradations.

Traditional	Something we've done historically.
Innovative for us	50%+ of competitors do this, not part of our current model.
Somewhat innovative	25–49% of competitors do this.
Fairly innovative	5–24% of competitors do this.
Highly innovative	0–4% of competitors do this.

The point is not whether 24 or 25 percent of rival entities pursue a given approach. Rather, this framework drives puzzlers to consider the relative novelty of proposals.

Ambitious Goals Ignite Imaginations

Amplified benchmarks and impressive positioning force puzzlers outside their comfort zones, catalyzing ambitious, unconventional thinking. Perhaps Criteria challenges them to:

- Become the STATE LEADER (when only citywide reputation has been considered)
- Become the COUNTRY LEADER (when only statewide reputation has been considered)
- Go VIRAL with 2 million hits
- Attract NATIONAL MEDIA coverage
- Win an AWARD no organization like us has received
- Get featured in the *Guinness Book of* WORLD RECORDS

Frame your GAME

with unambiguous **GUIDELINES** bound to inspire.

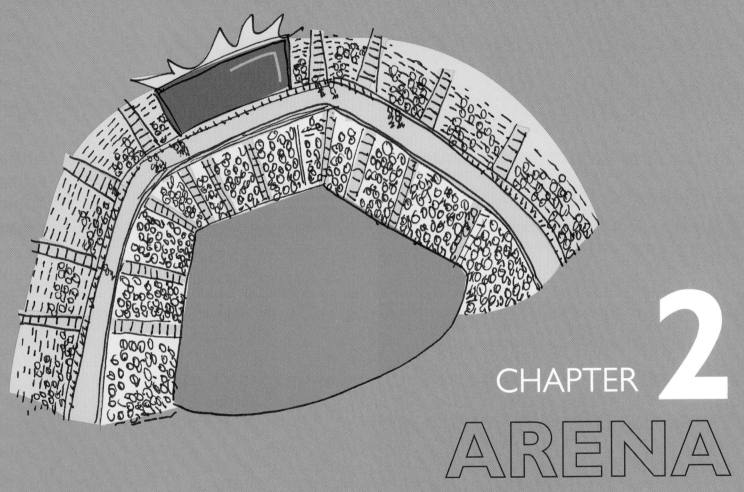

CHAPTER **2**

ARENA

Addressing the conditions you have to work with, an ARENA defines
your mix of problem solvers (**P**uzzlers), time frame (**P**eriod),
and physical/virtual environment (**P**lace).

What conditions?

ARENA

Upon entering an arena to watch American football, the game's results are uncertain.

Well before kickoff, however, unambiguous conditions are set. Each of two teams are allowed exactly 11 players on the field at a time. The hour-long game, divided into quarters, transpires on a 100-yard field flanked by end zones.

Similarly, when designing and playing GAMEs, the term *Arena* describes three critical aspects (**P**uzzlers, **P**eriod, **P**lace). Innovation champions optimize these conditions of play.

PUZZLERS —— **Who plays?**

PERIOD —— **What's the clock?**

PLACE —— **Where's the action?**

If you have the luxury of SELECTING AN ARENA, set Guidelines first. Then determine parameters:

The Arena is often OUT OF YOUR CONTROL. If so, design Guidelines considering the hand you've been dealt:

Puzzlers   Given the Challenge, what's the ideal team makeup?

Period   How much time is reasonably necessary?

Place   To maximize success, where's is the ideal venue?

Puzzlers   Which challenge(s) is your team most equipped to solve?

Period   Within the time frame, how big/complex a puzzle can be tackled?

Place   How might we maximize the chosen venue's potential?

"We cannot change the cards we are dealt, just how we play the hand."

—Randy Pausch, American author of
The Last Lecture

Puzzlers
Who plays?

The composition of a problem-solving army impacts creative capacity, community culture, logistical complexity, potential to delegate, and the ultimate solution. Swapping just one or two foot soldiers may result in major outcome differences.

You often have no control. Determined by the boss or fate, collaborators include coworkers, board members, folks trapped in the elevator. In such cases, don't spend a moment wishing things were different. Instead, play your best GAME with the puzzlers on hand.

Your people are the right people.

If you have the authority, however, curate this community wisely. Not all teams are equal. In fact, no two are alike.

Recruit the collection of puzzlers most likely to crack your code.

Carefully consider:

1. How many teams?

2. How many per team?

3. What team makeup?

 # Size Implications

SOLOIST
1 person

The smallest puzzling "team" is an unaccompanied act of one. Working alone offers flexibility, self-pacing, and ample room to reflect. Without opposing viewpoints, only personal limitations hold you back. Soloists are particularly well suited for nuts and bolts detail work.

TEAM
2–10 people

Even a single partner transforms the GAME, bringing affirmation, critique, ideas, motivation, and accountability. Each new associate augments variety and possibility, just as ingredients added to a base dish generate rich new taste. Increasingly delicious (and sometimes spicy) viewpoints flavor the gumbo. As teams expand, potential and imagination grow, while intimacy and podium time diminish.

MULTITEAM
independent groups

With multiple teams or rival individuals, it is possible to simultaneously breed contrasting solutions. Proposals can battle for adoption or be synthesized. Competitive formats are often motivational. Healthy environments stimulate positive peer pressure.

LEAGUE
large communities

Once a group grows beyond 10 or so, detailed collaboration becomes unwieldy. Large crowds produce profound imbalance, dominated by a few. But quantity works in your favor for certain tasks. Leagues are efficient when explaining challenges, cultivating skills, vetting ideas, asking for help, and building consensus.

Solo Problems, Team Solutions

Most individuals assume that personal challenges must be solved single-handedly. Recruiting help somehow *feels* inappropriate. After all, it's MY problem. It's MY job.

Sometimes this solo arrangement makes sense. But it does not inherently serve self-interest.

Teams are often better than soloists.

Being charged with something doesn't mean you alone must do the solving. There is power in numbers.

 CHALLENGE: Design a meaningful professional development day.

HR manager Percy Nell, tasked with organizing this event, understands that improving morale is the top priority. While he can certainly invite lecturers (something that's generated grumbles in the past), a hands-on, engaging experience is preferable.

Unfortunately, hours of pondering generate little more than frustration. To be honest, event planning isn't Percy's strong suit. But what can he do? "It's my job!" he curses.

And then an idea emerges. Percy invites a handful of coworkers from various departments to play a "GAME" around this challenge. Surprisingly, all are intrigued and sign up immediately.

Collaboration feels entirely different than isolation.

More brains mean more potential. Together, they build upon one another's ideas, imagining directions that never would have dawned on Percy alone. The process is fun, productive, and—unexpectedly—builds a sense of camaraderie. "How's that for a clue? . . ." he reflects.

The team ultimately advocates to organize this development day as an innovation GAME, tackling an important organizational challenge.

"Alone we can do so little. Together we can do so much."

—Helen Keller, American disability rights advocate

The following chart compares leadership requirements, suitability of activities, and general advantages/disadvantages of various sized problem-solving communities.

	Soloist	Team	Multiteam	League
LEADERSHIP	You alone control the agenda	Small groups: no formal leader required As size increases, appoint a captain	Option 1: Single "GAME master" for community Option 2: Each team has own captain	Skilled facilitator necessary at all times
BEST SUITED	Quiet time and introspection Detail work and logistical planning Challenges that draw on personal expertise	Brainstorm, test, and build creative ideas Accomplish a lot quickly, with limited red tape Delegate tasks	Same as individual team strengths Develop multiple concepts simultaneously	Disseminate content Test ideas Solicit help Vote on/tweak existing proposals Build consensus and momentum
LESS SUITED	Tasks that don't match expertise, interest, or skills Highly creative solutions Delegation and feedback	Quiet time Tasks better handled by individuals	Same as individual team weaknesses	Detail work Hands-on collaboration Creative visioning

	Soloist	Team	Multiteam	League
ADVANTAGES	Autonomous and efficient Work at your own pace Decisions without bureaucracy No interpersonal conflict/underperforming members	Social bonding All voices can be heard on small teams Accountability Balance strengths, weaknesses, skills Healthy debate, honest feedback	Generate multiple, diverse solutions Proposals can compete or be fused Teams learn from others Competitive environments inspire ambition	Access to many perspectives Efficiency, as shared ideas reach many ears Break into smaller groups
DISADVANTAGES	Everything falls on one person Limited perspective without idea sharing Nobody to help when stuck, unmotivated, sick, or off track Often lonely and less fulfilling	Scheduling challenges Unequal commitment "Groupthink" Individual voices/ perspectives can get lost Interpersonal conflict	Logistical challenges coordinating many people Necessary activity time may vary across teams Not every proposal can be pursued Uneven experience from group to group	Can't elicit equitable feedback from all May encourage passivity Single dissenter can derail (if not managed) The larger the ship, the harder to steer

Nonpuzzler Participants

Innovation GAMEs regularly engage individuals beyond official problem solvers. Though guests are generally present during only part of the process, their impact can be astronomical.

GAME *master*

Neutral facilitator who guides a multiteam experience (see Chapter 10).

INTERVIEW *subjects*

Target users who provide personal perspectives and insights.

FEEDBACK *providers*

Reviewers who offer honest, objective critique.

EXPERT *consultants*

Mentors who give guidance.

JUDGES / *respondents*

Jurors responsible for evaluating and rating projects.

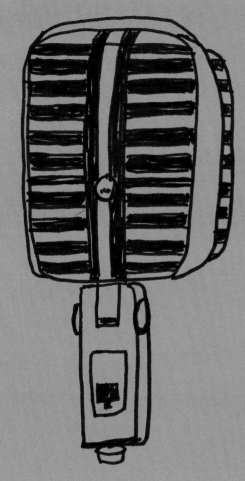

"Sometimes an outside perspective is the clearer perspective."

—Shannon A. Thompson, American author

Managing the Mix

In addition to team size, carefully consider the makeup of puzzlers. How diverse is the ideal combination?

When Homogeneous Teams Work Well

Most people are naturally drawn to others who look and think like them. There is comfort in sameness.

Worshippers find solidarity within their church, temple, or mosque. Millennials and seniors limit friendships to a single generation. Public schools, car dealerships, and barbershops investigate parallel entities for inspiration.

In most cases, this is no xenophobic exercise. Rather,

It feels safe and logical to associate with those who share similar backgrounds.

Homogeneous teams excel at puzzles suggesting the past, incremental change, or model replication. Drawing from a common reservoir of knowledge and discipline-specific jargon, everybody speaks the same language. Overwhelmingly unified worldviews streamline the process.

⭐ CHALLENGE: Open a nail salon.

In three short weeks, Manny Kyor will quit his job and move across the country. Following a long career as a beautician, his new life involves an exciting but intimidating proposition: opening a business.

With limited managerial experience, Manny convenes a group of colleagues to plot his business strategy. Invited precisely because of what they have in common, all are experienced parlor owners or managers. He banks on learning from their experience and wisdom.

When Diverse Teams Work Well

Homogeneous teams have a hard time recognizing core assumptions, let alone testing them. When expertise runs deep but narrow, it becomes difficult to see the world with fresh eyes. Conversations get trapped in the weeds. Conventional wisdom is taken as gospel.

Diverse teams, on the other hand, summon a larger set of skills and viewpoints. Puzzlers who intersect with the challenge in contrasting ways amplify creativity, knowledge base, and feedback potential.

Diversity is ideal for creative innovation challenges.

At times, everyone gets stuck while problem solving. However, different types of people struggle with different parts of the process. As a result, teams drawing from diverse perspectives are less likely to suffer a unilateral shutdown when confronting a hitch.

 **CHALLENGE: Revamp our irrigation system.**

The farmer Harvey Stur struggles to keep his crops alive and knows he needs help. To design an extraordinary, efficient solution, he convenes a problem-solving team.

Harvey quickly realizes that "farmers only" will be too limited. Hoping to explore a variety of uncommon directions, he invites a colorful assortment of characters offering unique perspectives.

The eventual roster includes a fellow agriculturalist, plumber, water engineer, aquarium builder, sculptor, chemist, and general creative with deep problem-solving expertise.

When Too Little Diversity Fails

Emphasizing their commitment to equity, diversity, and inclusion (EDI), many groups actively recruit historically marginalized, underrepresented populations. Despite admirable intentions, however, even these efforts can fall short.

Different-looking, same-thinking becomes the community.

Diversity entails more than race and gender. Think holistically when assembling puzzlers. Consider:

- Age
- Gender/sexual orientation
- Job title/rank/sector
- Neighborhood/geography
- Personal/professional experience
- Political/social views
- Race/ethnicity/religion
- Skill sets
- Socioeconomic strata
- Thinking styles (e.g., big vs. small picture orientation)
- Topic expertise

CHALLENGE: How might our company become more relevant and sustainable?

If nothing changes, Theo Speeyon fears his theater troupe may be run out of business. His puzzling team *looks* fairly diverse, blending men and women of different races. All theater professionals, they share a deep awareness of industry challenges and are committed to sustaining Theo's beloved organization.

Their GAME starts with a bang. Enthusiasm flows. But after a while, puzzlers hit a wall. The best suggestions mimic other (struggling) companies. Investigating beyond this familiar paradigm proves challenging.

Theo realizes he may have made a mistake. *Might voices from other sectors offer fresher ideas?* For example, a sports stadium thrives down the road. "What do they know that we don't?" he wonders.

"Inclusion is not a matter of political correctness. It is the key to growth."

—Jesse Jackson, American activist, minister, and politician

When Too Much Diversity Fails

In recent years, hype for diverse teams has exploded. Hailed as the secret to all of life's woes, this formula has indeed generated the remarkable. But that is far from guaranteed.

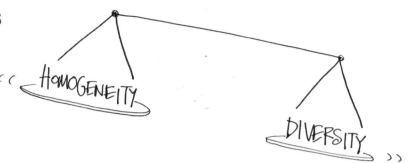

Diversity is not a panacea.

The benefits of diversity are available only when puzzlers are open to new ways of thinking. Intersecting fields or backgrounds lengthen the learning curve. Interpersonal challenges are introduced when puzzlers act insensitively or are unaware of emotional triggers.

There is such a thing as too much diversity.

When seven theories compete for attention, teams may become mired in differences, failing to agree on anything. Bitter disagreement on basic facts, premises, or priorities leads to gridlock and frustration.

It would be foolish for someone needing a back operation to consult a panel of dermatologists, stockbrokers, and hairdressers. Skilled surgeons are best equipped to solve this particular puzzle.

Stick with the experts.

CHALLENGE: Identify community priorities.

Urban developer Ar Katekt is looking to build a welcoming new neighborhood.

To imagine an oasis that energizes a rich array of demographics, Ar's puzzlers include an Asian college sophomore, Black father of young twins, Mexican retiree, Turkish wealthy businesswoman, white starving artist, and Jewish rancher.

At first, the diversity is incredible. Collectively, they propose all sorts of wonderful fantasies. The dad loves playgrounds. The artist advocates murals. The student wants taverns. The pensioner needs quiet.

When time comes to prioritize, however, no one will budge. Their wishes are too different. With little mood for compromise, this "community for all" starts feeling like a district for nobody.

The Best Experts

Innovation teams are clearly better off with intelligent, positive, invested contributors. Beyond that, the ideal mix depends on the puzzle itself.

CHALLENGE B

How might the company website become more compelling?

Quite different from the previous challenge, this is about intrigue, buzz, and meeting users on their turf.

In addition to IT support, a diverse team might include employees from across the organization as well as external consultants with fresh eyes. How about actual customers?

CHALLENGE A

Recode the company website to be sleeker and faster.

Though this may well involve creative strategizing, it calls primarily for technical expertise.

When it comes to skill sets, a fairly homogenous crew of designers and developers makes sense.

CHALLENGE C

Improve employee retention.

This challenge is typically addressed by upper management.

But why not include a variety of profiles such as entry-level employees, commuters, nursing moms, late-career workers, and so on?

Or a crazier idea: Folks who recently left the company. In addition to offering valuable insights and feedback, they are likely to broadcast leadership's sincere interest in making things better.

Consider the problem-under-the-problem.

CHALLENGE D

Revise the university English curriculum.

This team is obvious: *the language faculty*. They own the courses. They teach them. Case closed!

But hold on . . . why is revision necessary in the first place?

If a discontinued textbook must be replaced, English teachers are key.

But what if the world has changed, yet higher education hasn't kept up?

What if the goal is to teach *students* rather than English, preparing them for fulfilling lives and viable careers? In this case, a broader coalition is advisable. Identify an array of puzzlers who bring unique value to the GAME.

• English professors who teach the courses

• Other faculty with transferrable ideas

• Administrators with a solid grasp of university goals

• Representative students with insights on what motivates peers

• Career coaches or business leaders who understand workforce needs

"A lot of different flowers make a bouquet."

—Islamic proverb

Period
What's the clock?

Problem solving requires time.

Yet in a world where people confront seemingly infinite projects, many important challenges are deprived the minutes they deserve. With everyone so busy, how can we reasonably carve out room for *this*?

As a result, vital steps are rushed or neglected altogether. Innovation is sacrificed. Important issues are moved indefinitely to the back burner.

Time is the scarcest resource. Be careful never to waste it. But skimp here at your own risk.

There is always enough time for what matters most.

Innovation GAMEs are played on many timelines. In selecting one, carefully consider what can reasonably be accomplished within the allocated period.

Necessary Time Frame

How long does it take to complete a project?

I've posed this query to many groups. The response is predictable: "Depends what you have to do!"

But I respectfully disagree. Most of us use exactly the same amount of time to get just about anything done.

. . . As long as you have.

If the assignment is due next week, final touches are added the night before. Given a month or a season, it similarly comes together at the 11th hour. And if there's a year—you get the point.

The exception goes to planners with extended deadlines. When projecting three, five, ten years down the road, their vision is unlikely to ever be realized.

Not enough urgency!

The trick to planning a GAME, or anything else for that matter, is reserving just enough time.

Three sagacious words transform productivity:

Deadlines with consequences.

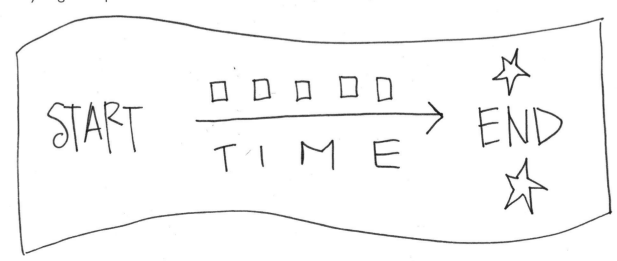

Short, medium, and long GAME examples are included in Chapter 4.

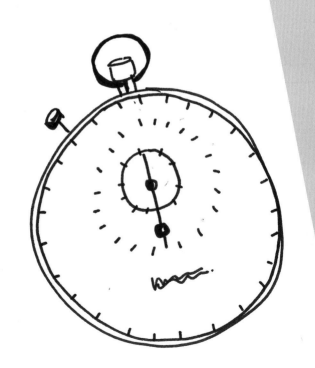

Short GAME: **Sprint**

Duration: 30 minutes to 2 hours

Short GAMEs, playable during typical meeting periods, are all you need to start solving problems. While too brief to flesh out complex solutions, this period is nonetheless sufficient for meaningful, self-contained experiences.

One possibility is honing in on a Sector Solution (page 47), or small part of the problem. Another involves harvesting large-scale concepts to be developed later.

Or the goal can be to simply cultivate skills and build community. Regardless of scope, the key is designing a stand-alone process where *something* tangible is achieved before the closing bell.

Even sprints can generate valuable outcomes.

Medium GAME: **Jog**

Duration: Half to full day (typically 3–10 hours)

Unlike sprints, medium GAMEs require a special event. The focal point of retreats, development days, and conferences, they allow more opportunity for exploration and strategizing.

Within the course of a jog, puzzlers can reasonably develop a skeletal prototype and/or proposal. There may be time for outside voices to make cameos (interview subjects, expert consultants, etc.).

Rather than covering too much ground, stay focused.

Deeper is better than wider.

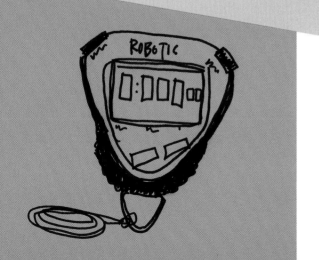

Long GAME: **Marathon**

2 days to 1 week (or longer)

It is amazing how much can be accomplished during marathons. When done well, these immersive experiences unleash the extraordinary.

Individual phases may span hours, allowing ample time for detective work, prototype development, feedback collection, consensus building, and other activities.

Marathons are exhilarating and intense.

Pay special attention to the emotional trajectory. Demands of play can wear on individuals over time, though everyone responds differently. Some commit to positivity, while others get skittish. Puzzlers typically begin relaxed and good-humored, and most teams finish strong. But in between, extended concentration and GAME demands may trigger prickly personalities.

Facilitators should stay keenly attuned to team dynamics.

 Other Meets

Blocking out an uninterrupted time period to play an innovation GAME is not always possible. Here are additional scheduling options.

	Overview	Time Frame	Strength	Challenge
PERIODIC RACES	Series of sprints (self-contained GAMEs or continuing effort)	Meets weekly, monthly, or sporadically	Cumulative time Reflect between meetings	Maintaining momentum
RELAYS	Different teams address different parts of the problem Hand off solutions	Flexible, as often as time allows	Accountable to a deadline Each team makes a unique contribution	Building continuity Communication and cohesion between teams
COUNTDOWNS	Must solve by prescribed date Meet and work as necessary	Combine sprints, jogs, and/or marathons	More perspectives Time commitment is more flexible	Not waiting until the last minute Committing enough time and energy
OPEN-ENDED	Work until puzzle is solved	Flexible	No real or artificial deadline Continue until a great solution emerges	Lacks urgency Time management Hard to prioritize
HYBRIDS	Combination of above	Flexible	Integrated approach advantages	Integrated approach weaknesses

Polly Sea has been assigned to oversee a daunting exercise.

 # CHALLENGE: **Revise the employee handbook (last updated: 1982).**

Chairing a committee of nine puzzlers representing every department, she has their undivided attention for 75-minutes per week over the course of three months.

Rather than treating this as a single gigantic puzzle, her *periodic races* involve a series of independent GAMEs. Each engaging, carefully planned experience tackles one isolated aspect.

During week one, they determine which issues to include in the new document. Subsequent meetings outline priority points for identified "chapters": employee benefits, promotion guidelines, conflict resolution, anti-discimination policies, technology protocols, and so on.

Between sessions, a selected puzzler is tasked with typing up specific language, to be discussed briefly the next time they convene.

After the final GAME, Polly collates and wordsmiths team contributions, ensuring a consistent voice throughout. She is grateful not only for assistance with this time-consuming work, but also with the positive outcome of buy-in thanks to collaborative visioning.

"Time isn't the main thing.
It's the only thing."

—Miles Davis, American jazz trumpeter

PLACE
Where's the action?

Perhaps no resource is as universally squandered as physical space.

Even multinational corporations with architectural marvels fail this test, at least if they aspire to innovation. Sure, the office is nice. *But walls are bare or boring.* Artwork is limited to CEO portraits and random imagery. An eerie formality punishes creativity, as visitors tiptoe to avoid spilling coffee on the proverbial Persian rug.

Rooms are more than inconsequential square footage. They impact process, psychology, even outcomes.

What story does yours tell?

Space matters!

Kindergarten teachers have figured this out. They understand the value—necessity—of celebrating community members while showcasing exploration. Who needs Rembrandts when we've got dioramas and sock puppets designed by our very own creative geniuses?

A little imagination goes a long way.

It can transform hideous spaces, or even beautiful ones, into vibrant experimentation laboratories.

Venue Sets the Stage

When choosing locales, consider how practical implications will impact your GAME. Is it accessible? How many people fit? Which rooms are available? What technology? Wall space? Seating? Food options? Restrictions?

Foreign Offsite locations unleash fresh energy, adding gravitas to the experience.	VS.	**Familiar** People know how to get there, find bathrooms, use the technology.
Bohemian Unconventional venues may inspire novel thinking.	VS.	**Bare** Basic rooms provide a backdrop that can be unobtrusive or reimagined.
Unified Challenge-related locations (e.g., farm when discussing agribusiness) allow puzzlers to engage directly with the problem.	VS.	**Unrelated** Perhaps all you need is a neutral space.
Costly Fancy, expensive locations offer puzzlers a sweet reward for their efforts.	VS.	**Complementary** Free/inexpensive venues leave money for other activities. This may be the only viable option.

⭐ CHALLENGE: Draft a meaningful criminal justice reform bill.

To do this, Judy Shurry will lead a team of lawyers and lawmakers.

Rather than meeting in the usual downtown highrise, she opts for a less traditional setting. Emphasizing the urgency surrounding this issue, they convene in a prison.

Seating Impacts Engagement

When nothing is bolted to the ground, you control how teams engage. Seating formation impacts activities, conversations, and collaborations. Choose one arrangement, or alternate during various phases.

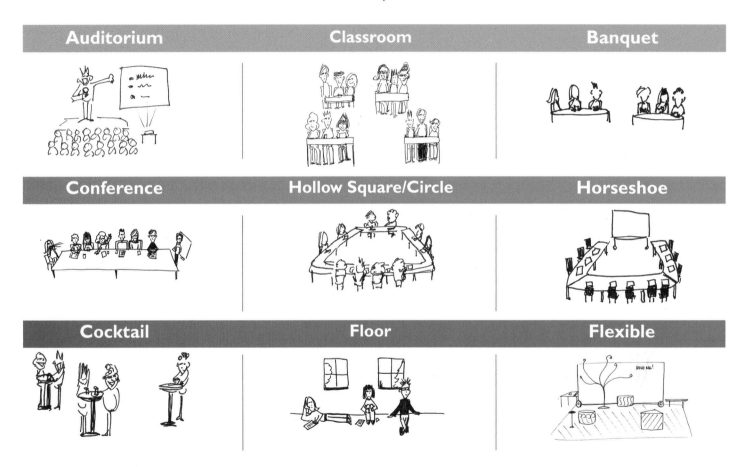

When left to their own devices, puzzlers notoriously gravitate to familiar faces or those with similar backgrounds, particularly in large groups. To force unlikely connections, mix things up by strategically assigning seats. When that is impractical, instruct folks to join forces with those they don't yet know.

Décor Inspires Action

Transport puzzlers to an alternate reality as they enter your GAME.

When that happens, a pleasant shock often beams through their eyes as if to suggest, "WOW, this is cool! We must have important work to do."

Evoking magic mustn't require much, particularly for those new to innovation. Most people operate in realms where creative space making is largely absent. Birthday parties, yes. Problem solving, no.

Some venues are breathtaking, others hip, still others drab. Regardless of intrinsic aesthetics, any space can be transformed with a little planning and creativity.

Consider potential within, and leave ample time for setup.

Organize your puzzling space like a work of art.

Paint the Walls

Walls, columns, and other structural elements are commonly integrated as:

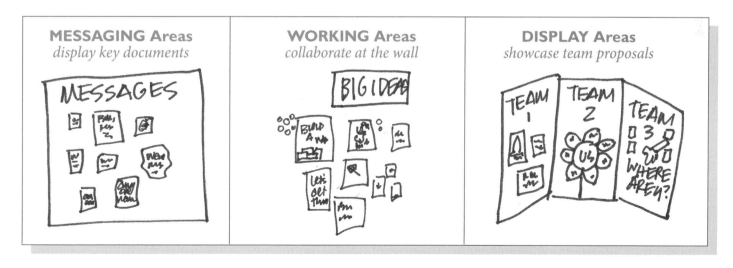

MESSAGING Areas
display key documents

WORKING Areas
collaborate at the wall

DISPLAY Areas
showcase team proposals

Set the Table

More than mere sitting spots, tables become a canvas for exploration, displaying vital Materials (Chapter 3).

Tables are opportunities.

Take great care when "setting the table." Give your GAME a look, considering the placement and aesthetics of each item. Pay attention to details, even the direction of pens or Post-it pad stacks.

For multiple stations, begin with a prototype table and then unify the setup.

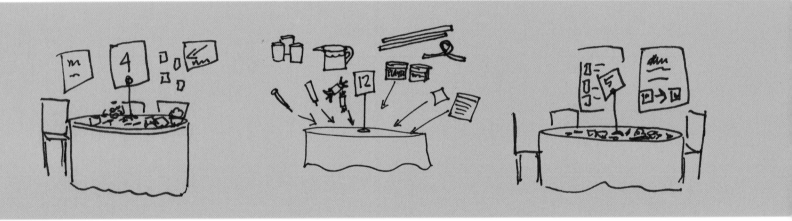

Establish a Focal Point

Where will attention be centered? Consider the sightline from various locations. The decision may be made if a screen is required. Rotating focal points adds variety, but creates logistical challenges.

Team Spaces Help Groups Blossom

Many GAMEs involve multiple teams working in the same large chamber, each assigned their own table. Doing so makes it possible to switch seamlessly between independent teamwork and full community discussion.

A presiding facilitator—known as a *GAME master*—typically guides the process, roams the space, and addresses questions. Participants learn by observing one another, finding motivation in collective energy.

In addition to this central location, it may be helpful to offer groups their own real estate for at least parts of the process.

Common practice during long GAMEs, doing so permits increased freedom and autonomy.

Just be sure puzzlers clearly grasp instructions when working independently.

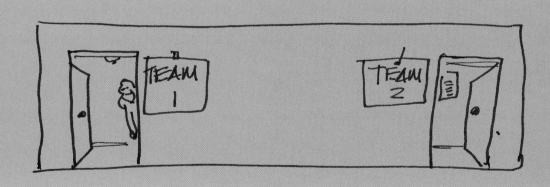

Each space becomes an independent universe.

It is fascinating to observe competing team rooms. Different leadership and collaboration styles emerge. Some groups stay unwaveringly serious, while others are less formal. Creativity on display is astounding, as communities explore their own unique voices.

GAMEing Online

In-person GAMEs offer many perks. Multiple teams learn from one another. Distributing materials is a breeze. Riveting conversations occur by accident thanks to impromptu coffee station gatherings. The room's energy is discernible.

But this is not the only possibility. Video conferencing options have exploded, catapulted by an international pandemic that temporarily made virtual meetings the only responsible setting.

When designing online GAMEs, do not present a less good version of face-to-face. Instead,

Capitalize on the unique benefits of your platform.

Lean into technology. Play to its strengths. Deemphasize weaknesses. While there will be continuous improvement, here are some benefits already available.

Simplified logistics: No need to secure or pay for physical facilities.

No parking/commute: Anyone, anywhere can participate, saving time and money.

Easily record: Just press a button to capture sessions, no extra equipment required.

Name tags: Most platforms clearly showcase names, making it simple to identify even strangers.

Visibility: In person, folks far away scramble to see. Online, everyone has a close-up view.

Hearability: In person, participants struggle to hear soft, unamplified voices. Online, everyone has their own mic—just be sure they are optimized and unmuted at the right time!

Shareability: It is unwieldy to view work-in-progress from across a large space. Online, anyone can easily share their screen.

Room switch: In person, there are invariably stragglers when moving from breakout rooms to a central location. Online, the process can be automated.

Chat: All puzzlers can be asked to display thoughts simultaneously, rather than just the first one who raises a hand. Or individuals can communicate privately without disturbing others. Or comments are instantly shared with everyone. Just be clear about protocols so this feature helps rather than distracts.

Technology can be amazing when it works, infuriating when it doesn't. For experiences involving large groups or complexity, engage 1–2 people whose sole role is technological oversight. Requiring a facilitator or puzzler to play double duty diminishes the experience for everyone.

Schedule a pre-event tech rehearsal. In my experience, anything untested is likely to go wrong. To avoid that frustration and time suck, test visual/audio sharing in advance. Determine how breakout rooms are assigned.

Rehearse the integration of supplemental software. Aim for a seamless experience.

Emphasize ground rules as your event begins. Request that cameras remain on at all times, since it is virtually (excuse the pun) impossible to equally engage "invisible" puzzlers. Articulate microphone policy, how to access materials, participation protocols, and so on. Most important, emphasize the need to turn off outside life.

Insist that puzzlers be 100% present throughout.

LOOK YOUR BEST

Comb hair, choose a nice nondistracting shirt, wear pants.

CLEAR THE BACKGROUND

Show yourself, not your stuff! Favor simple backdrops.

"FRONT LIGHT" YOUR FACE

Avoid side or back light. Don't sit in front of a window.

BACK OFF

Too close to the camera is creepy. Position yourself at a distance.

LOOK INTO THE CAMERA

Make "eye contact." Looking elsewhere feels uncomfortable.

USE AN EXTERNAL MIC

Even cheap options work wonders. Mute when not talking.

■ Whatever the dimensions of your **ARENA**, make the most of resources at hand.

CHAPTER **3**

MATERIALS

MATERIALS, the tools of innovation, include a variety of supplies (**G**atherables), specialty game items (**G**ear), and mapping canvases (**G**ameboards).

What tools?

MATERIALS

A thimble is no wheelbarrow! The opposite is true as well. Each object offers distinct value. Equally of note, they trigger unique mental processing.

Tools matter.

Game companies develop sophisticated products that combine tactile engagement with varied activity. Some games require boards. Many incorporate specialty objects (cards, dice, chips, figurines).

The best components focus energy while igniting imagination.

Similarly, when designing GAMEs, innovation champions explore a range of items (**G**atherables, **G**ear, **G**ameboards).

Weighing psychological and practical implications, the choice between Post-it or whiteboard, ballpoint or Sharpie, is consequential. Each brings unique pros and cons, impacting thought process, creative potential, and ultimate outcome.

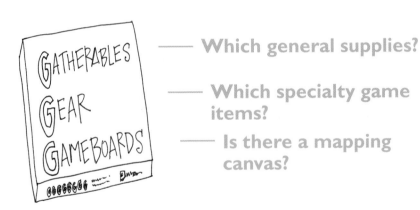

—— **Which general supplies?**

—— **Which specialty game items?**

—— **Is there a mapping canvas?**

"A good tool improves the way you work.

A great tool improves the way you think."

—Jeff Duntemann, American writer and contrarian

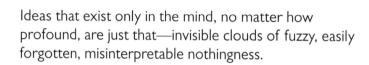

Gatherables

Which general supplies?

Gatherables, the raw materials of problem solving, are readily available and often inexpensive.

Build your arsenal over time.

Writing Implements
Differentiate Content

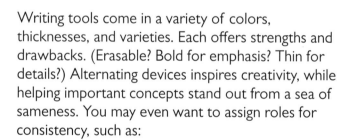

Writing tools come in a variety of colors, thicknesses, and varieties. Each offers strengths and drawbacks. (Erasable? Bold for emphasis? Thin for details?) Alternating devices inspires creativity, while helping important concepts stand out from a sea of sameness. You may even want to assign roles for consistency, such as:

• **Sharpies** for headlines
• **Ballpoints/pencils** for clarifying
• **Highlighters** for emphasis
• **Crayons/markers** for images

Ideas that exist only in the mind, no matter how profound, are just that—invisible clouds of fuzzy, easily forgotten, misinterpretable nothingness.

Only when codified in writing or pictures can concepts be effectively shared, remembered, studied, organized, and examined from multiple angles.

Inviting puzzlers to notate their own ideas gets everyone active, but increases the likelihood that folks temporarily tune out.

A single designated *scribe* offers consistency and frees others from multitasking. However, unskilled transcribers slow the process, and missed/misinterpreted comments may be gone forever.

It often makes sense to appoint a *doodler* as well, charged with communicating through images.

Experiment to see which system works best.

MARKER

BALLPOINT

SHARPIE

PENCIL

DRY ERASE MARKER

CHALK

CRAYONS

Small Paper Keeps Ideas Flexible

Small paper is the tool of choice for capturing independent ideas.

Whether distributing index cards around a table or adhering sticky notes to the wall, entries can easily be:

ADDED	SUBTRACTED	SHUFFLED	GROUPED

 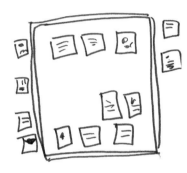 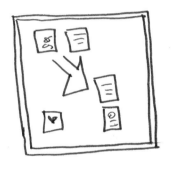 

It's a common scene. Puzzlers staring at a wall packed with Post-its are challenged to identify promising concepts.

Unfortunately, outstanding contenders get buried or are overlooked completely.

Presentation matters.

Visual elements communicate more than words alone. Hopefully, this book makes that abundantly clear.

You needn't be Picasso to employ effective visual communication. Even stick figures, simple sketches, and basic color variation convey energy.

Use Sharpies or other thick markers for title concepts, adding supplemental details with pencil or ballpoint.

Attractive entries feature LARGE legible writing, catchy headlines, and few words.

Bold ideas deserve bold fonts.

Compelling content pops off the page.

To maximize small paper's flexibility, add just the right amount of information.

Middle school book reports with required word counts taught many of us the art of verbosity. Now it's time to forget those nostalgic lessons.

Too much writing dilutes your message. Delete the extraneous while succinctly capturing its essence. Less is almost always more.

When possible, limit core concepts to 1–4 words.

CHALLENGE: Level up your leadership.

When brainstorming important attributes of leaders, a group of CEOs made Post-it points like:

- Great leaders show moral courage in hard times.
- Great leaders are passionate about what they do.
- Great leaders empower their community by giving them a role.

Good observations, indeed. But at 8–10 words apiece, the writing process slows and "fonts" get small.

Asked to tighten things up, revisions include:

- Moral courage in hard times
- Passionate about their work
- Their empowering communities invite inclusion

Better! Possible to make points shorter yet?

- Moral Courage
- Passion
- Inclusive & Empowering

Bravo!

"Verbosity wastes a portion of the reader's or listener's life."

—Mokokoma Mokhonoana, South African mystic, philosopher, social critic

Large Surfaces Offer Idea Storage

Where small paper forces brevity, large surfaces invite exploration.

Expansive areas offer ample room to notate numerous entries and work through complex puzzles. Placed on walls, tables, easels, and floors, puzzlers may choose to stand, sit, or crouch while populating content.

A chosen surface and how it is used influence thinking.

Surface	*Core Benefit*
Whiteboards, Chalkboards, Glass Boards	Erasable
Flip Charts	Multiple sheets hung around room and kept for reference; write on directly or adhere Post-its
Butcher Paper	Unrolled to virtually any length
Poster Boards	Sturdy, ideal when writing directly on surface or attaching items
Notebooks, Worksheets, Loose-Leaf Pages	For individual notetakers

Some puzzlers project logical organization, with symmetrical gridlike lists. Others display nonlinear streams of consciousness, juxtaposing entries of every color, size, and direction.

There is no "right" way. If you get stuck or want to shake things up, try another approach.

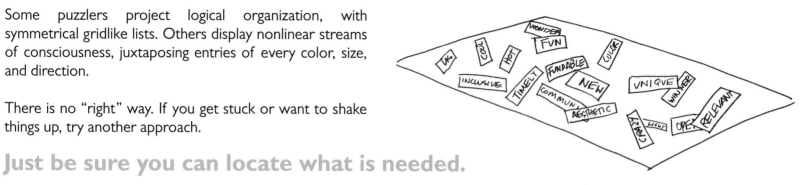

Just be sure you can locate what is needed.

 ## Adhesives Make Ideas Sticky

Materials like glues and tapes attach articles to walls or other objects.

Adhesive	*Use*
GLUES (glue pastes, glue sticks, glue guns)	Most are (semi-) permanent, geared toward certain types of materials.
TAPES (scotch, masking, painter's, double sided, etc.)	Various sizes, colors, and strengths. *(Caution: Only use painter's tape on delicate façades.)*
DRAFTING DOTS (precut tape dots)	For attaching notecards to fragile surfaces.
STICKERS (variety of shapes and sizes)	Effective voting tools (e.g., place on favorite Post-it)
STICKY WALL (like butcher paper, but sticky on both sides)	One of my favorite inventions, allows paper items to be affixed directly to its surface!

Prototyping Supplies Bring Ideas to Life

For processes that involve prototyping (page 216), an array of additional Materials can be helpful:

Art supplies	Crayons	Paints	Rulers
Bags (plastic/paper)	Electronic materials	Paper cutter	Scissors
Balls	Fabrics	Paperclips	Specialty papers
Blocks	Felt	Pencil sharpener	Stapler
Boxes	Glitter	Pipe cleaners	Staples
Buckets	Hammers, pliers,	Plastic silverware	Stencils
Cardboard	screwdrivers, etc.	Play-doh	Straws
Circuitry	Hardware (nails, etc.)	Printers	String
Clamps	LED lights	Q-tips	Tin foil
Coffee stirrers	Legos	Recycled containers	Toilet paper rolls
Construction paper	Metals	Ribbons	Wood
Cotton balls	Paintbrushes	Rubber bands	Yarn

Technology Can Help or Hurt

Technology plays a variety of roles in innovation GAMEs.

TAKE NOTES for editable, sharable records	**PROJECT SLIDES** and important data
DESIGN PROTOTYPES and other digital images	**PHOTOGRAPH WORK** for future scanning
RECORD CONVERSATION so nothing gets lost	**VIDEO CONFERENCE** with remote locations
SHARE DOCUMENTS through cloud services	**SUBMIT IDEAS** or vote with social media

Exclusive reliance on technology brings drawbacks.

Typing has a hard time unlocking preschool-level creativity, particularly when competing against crayons, chalk, or colored paper. If one person inputs to a personal screen, others are deprived of the visual reference. Projections limit viewable content, a stark contrast to 15 flip charts strewn about the space. Unwanted beeps and status notifications are distracting.

These solvable issues are mentioned to make a point. Many puzzlers dismiss analog tools as naïve and unnecessary. But that perspective is unfortunate.

Tech-heads are well served when expanding their bag of tricks, working shoulder to shoulder with colleagues using tangible Materials.

And to Luddites:

The potential of tech is too powerful to ignore.

Gear

Which specialty game items?

Specialty GAME items contribute to a fun, playful atmosphere. Just as significantly, well designed Gear alters thinking and outcomes in profound ways.

Detail Docs Add Clarity

Detail documents, distributed as the GAME begins or when they become necessary, clarify and reinforce.

WORKSHEETS

Completable forms

Provides timings, directives, and response fields, articulating what is expected.

Particularly for online or multiroom GAMEs, it may be helpful to create worksheets outlining each activity.

POSTERS and HANDOUTS

Visual references

May contain: Guidelines, maps, rules, background details, resources, other helpful information.

Post around room or give copies to teams.

Avatars Bring Subjects to Life

Your challenge may be to help hundreds, thousands, even millions of people. But it's difficult to design solutions for the masses. Rather than attempting to address a scope so large:

Identify the single hero of your challenge.

Like a video gamer, genetically engineer an *avatar*, complete with name and backstory. Model this persona after your ideal consumer, user, partner, constituent. Such characters often combine traits from multiple humans.

During play, imagine stunning solutions for this central character.

If your strategy works, it will undoubtedly resonate with a broader population.

When multiple groups must be targeted, play the GAME several times, changing avatars each round. Or assign contrasting characters to independent teams. Later in the process, you can consider whether and how innovations transfer to multiple audiences.

Bring avatars to life with their very own BIO, emphasizing relevant data and clues.

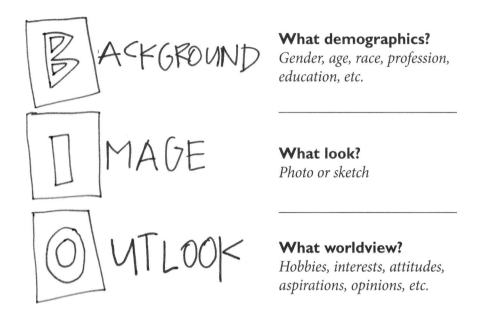

What demographics?
Gender, age, race, profession, education, etc.

What look?
Photo or sketch

What worldview?
Hobbies, interests, attitudes, aspirations, opinions, etc.

★ CHALLENGE: Create a bike-friendly environment.

Motor Rage City hopes to improve local traffic, safety, and quality of life. Weeks before running their bike-centric innovation GAME, city leadership interviews several neighbors. Hoping to better understand the community, they inquire about hobbies and habits, needs and wants.

Based on observations, a series of avatars are created to represent hypothetical riders.

Note how sample BIOs on the next page offer succinct points about Background and Outlook. While not every entry will ultimately prove instructive, the hope is that several offer meaningful clues.

During play, each team is assigned a different profile and challenged to conceive an exciting bike-related initiative that benefits their persona.

MIKE

Biking Advocate

Background

Mid-40s
Single, gay
Korean
Owns bicycle repair shop

Image

Outlook

Die-hard for the cause

Bike rides everywhere, thinks
everyone should

Frequently sponsors events

Politically active
(especially about biking)

Upset about lack
of bike trails

SHANIKA

Commuter

Background

27-year-old
Married, no kids
African-American
Chef

Image

Outlook

Wants to stay in shape

Cares about environment
and carbon footprint

Volunteers when possible

Pressed for time

ELLIE

Weekend Warrior

Background

Just turned 67
2 sons/5 grandkids
Retired, active
Well-off financially

Image

Outlook

Prioritizes exercise

Enjoys exploring various
neighborhoods

Loves parks, trails, animals

Encyclopedic knowledge of
area

Loves chatting with strangers

Timers Enforce Accountability

As we will see in Chapter 4, innovation GAMEs involve a sequence of timed activities, often enforced by an appointed timekeeper.

Various timing gizmos and alarms (indicating "time's up!") are available. While pragmatic in function, fun items contribute to a sense of play. It may be helpful for puzzlers to see countdowns projected onto a screen. If not, consider providing updates along the way (e.g., "3 minutes left").

Timing Gizmos:	Alarms:
windup timers	cymbals
sand timers	sirens
stopwatches	whistles
phones/tablets	random instruments
LED sports timers	electronic sounds
projections onto a screen	verbal commands

Though minutes per activity should be established in advance, it is often necessary to add or subtract time during play. Pay attention to team needs, weighing implications of change against the overall period.

★ CHALLENGE: Improve the waitroom experience.

Eternal Health Family Clinic is known for outstanding care and empathetic physicians. They also have a reputation for falling far behind schedule, creating long, irritating patient delays.

Team captain Ray Sing-Dreamer assigns each puzzler one concept to develop. Ultimately, they will have just 90 seconds apiece to pitch, providing crucial details and advocating merits.

Strict time limits force his loquacious colleagues to practice, get to the point, and avoid rambling. When finishing within the allocated window, puzzlers proudly indicate success by chiming a hotel bell. Straggling too long triggers the dreaded gong. Speakers must halt immediately, even midsentence.

Both fun and challenging, colleagues listen carefully, rooting for presenters to beat that danged timer.

Concept Cards Amplify Creative Thinking

Beyond adding a playful twist, customized playing cards* are particularly effective at challenging puzzlers to think in new ways. Here are a few examples of how they can be used.

IDEA GENERATION

When brainstorming, teams are given a stack of WHAT IF cards to inspire fresh thinking (e.g., What if your project involved: Robots? Bubbles? Virtual Reality?). After picking a card, jot down as many ideas as come to mind before choosing another. Repeat until time is up.

PRIORITY ALIGNMENT

Teams arrange two sets of identical cards from least to most important. The first row indicates *customer interests*. The second reveals how the *current business model* emphasizes these aspects. Finally, pieces of yarn connect top and bottom rows, indicating how well/poorly customer and business priorities align.

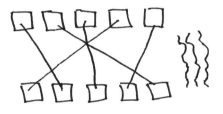

CONSTRAINTS

Drawing from a deck, each team picks three cards describing a value, feature, target audience, or other aspect that MUST be integrated into their proposal. Because no two cards are the same, a variety of solutions are guaranteed.

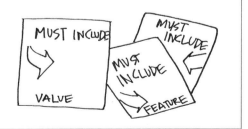

Cards are created by printing or drawing words and/or images onto index cards, blank playing cards, other small paper, or cardstock sheets (typically four to a page, to be cut and laminated).

 **CHALLENGE:**

Design an unforgettable holiday party.

When planning their upcoming event, Celebration Circus generates excitement through a card GAME.

A number of *concept cards*, each placed in a balloon before the GAME begins, describe potential themes: safari, roaring 20s, circus, space exploration, caving, the year 2100, and so on. Teams choose one at random to pop, determining their event's proposed focus.

Teams then draw three *feature cards* from a deck, identifying common party elements (e.g., meal, dessert, attire, music, speeches, table décor). Tying features to their concept, creative ideas are developed.

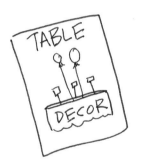  

The experience ends in friendly competition. Groups have three minutes to pitch their concept.

Before voting on favorites, everyone listens and laughs, moved by outrageous creativity.

Currency Makes It Real

Energy intensifies when money (poker chips, play dollars, actual cash) is involved. Currency can be used to:

VOTE	**BUDGET**	**PURCHASE**
show support for favorite idea(s)	allocate resources, stressing relative priorities and cash flow	"buy" GAME items (prototyping materials, consulting, etc.)

 CHALLENGE: How might we launch with a bang?

In anticipation of S. Presso's Café opening, the entire staff plays a GAME.

Six teams brainstorm their top five marketing strategies, along with cost projections. Maximum allowable budgets are delivered in sealed envelopes with play money. To inspire contrasting solutions, each group receives a different amount.

Team 1 finds an impressive $15,000. Team 2 gets 10 grand, and the sum decreases from there. Team 6 is granted just $22.47.

Interestingly, an inverse correlation between money and imagination becomes evident. Better funded teams identify fairly obvious, expensive solutions like TV and print advertising.

Those with less are exponentially more inventive, describing low-cost, high-imagination *guerilla tactics*.

For example, the lowest-funded team proposed novel concepts such as organizing a "caffeine parade" and inviting local celebrities to a "latte drink off."

Pickers Force Exploration

Even open-minded teams regularly gravitate to safe choices. Though not necessarily bad, they come at the expense of more intriguing directions.

When multiple puzzlers arrive at similar conclusions, they've either discovered gold or . . . *the obvious*. To avoid this phenomenon:

Let FATE choose.

Perhaps a team that is innovating customer service is presented with 20 aspects. Rather than selecting which parameter to reinvent, they roll a D20 (20-sided) die. If 17 comes up, the 17th entry is evaluated.

Pickers include standard dice (6-sided), nonstandard dice (4-, 8-, 10-, 12-, 16-, or 20-faces available), dice domes (containing multiple dice), spinners, roulette wheels, bingo drums, dominos, tops, and playing cards. This gear can be used to determine any number of issues. For example:

This Action	Determines This
Roll DICE	Duration (minutes) for a given activity
Spin ball on ROULETTE WHEEL	Quantity of ideas that must be generated
Pick a CARD	Which concept to explore (8 of hearts = 8th idea)
Draw letter from BINGO DRUM	Beginning letter for brainstormed concepts
Use a SPINNER	Who contributes next

Prizes Encourage Commitment

Prizes—whether anticipated or unannounced—add to a fun, competitive spirit. Accolades are commonly awarded toward the end of a GAME. But they can also be sprinkled throughout, honoring puzzlers who complete activities with flying colors (e.g., brainstorm the most entries).

Awards need not be luxurious.

A chocolate bar, specialty drink, trophy, gag gift, priority lunch line placement, pageant sash, or one million points (whatever that means) may be more than enough.

Gameboards

Is there a mapping canvas?

Not every GAME involves a board. But many do, and for good reason. The best Gameboards:

1. Define a clear framework for play

2. Guide the process

3. Invite a multitude of solutions

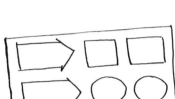

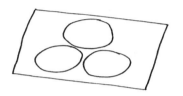

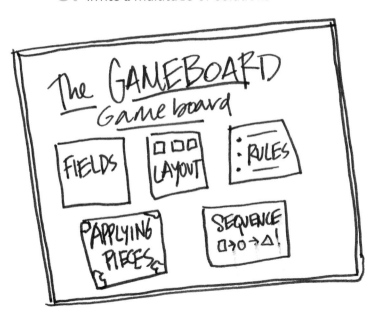

Innovation Gameboards are ideal for conceptualizing and showcasing comprehensive strategies. The object is to define multiple fields central to your challenge.

Doing so emphasizes the interrelatedness of elements, while simplifying even complex structures to their essence. Typically printed on large surfaces (24" × 36" or greater), details are added with Post-its or other small paper.

How might your strategy be reduced to a single page?

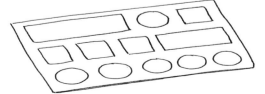

A Sample Canvas

In 2010, Alexander Osterwalder and Yves Pigneur rocked the business world with a novel proposition. Rather than writing a traditional, lengthy business plan, what if you boiled the vision down to a single page *Business Model Canvas?*

Divided into nine blocks indicating aspects crucial to every venture, this simple yet sophisticated tool has revolutionized how entrepreneurs, educators, and even multinational corporations conceptualize their scope and structure.

Value Proposition	Why do you matter?
Customer Segments	Who is your audience?
Customer Relationships	How do you engage clients?
Channels	How do you reach clients?
Key Partners	Who are essential collaborators?
Key Activities	Which tasks require attention?
Key Resources	Which assets do you offer?
Revenue Streams	How do you make money?
Cost Structure	How do you spend money?

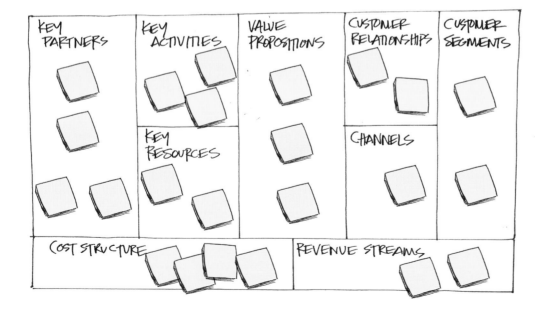

To complete the board, Post-it notes are added to appropriate fields. Indicating priorities, the trick is building/showcasing a cohesive strategy that is comprehensive yet manageable. Every entry represents a project, so include only what is necessary for success.

When done well, team members and external reviewers can quickly grasp a great deal about even complex business models. No more digging through endless pages of prose!

Build Your Own Board (BYOB)

While the Business Model Canvas represents a powerful set of organizational principles, it is just one approach to one problem. Your challenge may require different considerations altogether.

Why not design your own gameboard?

The Puzzler Company *New Venture Gameboard*, also geared toward entrepreneurial visioning, considers a different set of benchmarks.

Note how the sequence of fields is indicated with arrows. By guiding the process, this design helps puzzlers develop a logical structure and storyline.

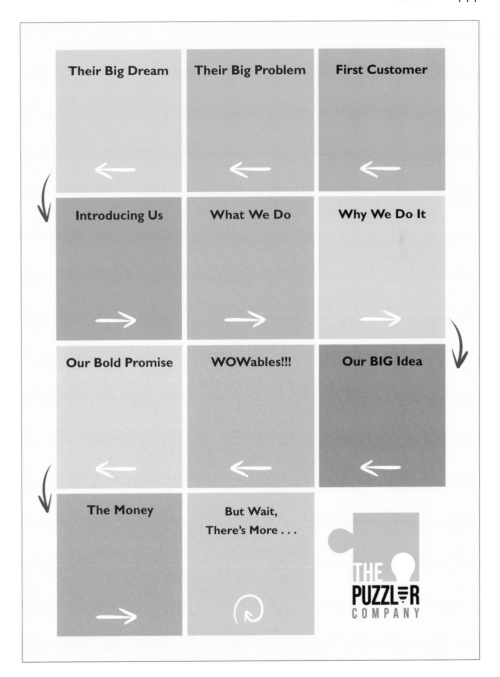

To create your own gameboard, begin by identifying large-scale parameters (typically 4–12) central to the challenge.

Which aspects must be defined to build a comprehensive success strategy?

Then design the layout. Beautiful, sophisticated graphic design is impressive, but crude, blocky drawings on flip charts also suffice. Be sure each field is large enough to accommodate multiple sticky notes.

 CHALLENGE: Determine the ideal location for our new corporate headquarters.

Following five years of exponential growth, Service Providers seeks the ideal home base. After considering many parameters, CEO Job Kreator designs a gameboard emphasizing seven priorities.

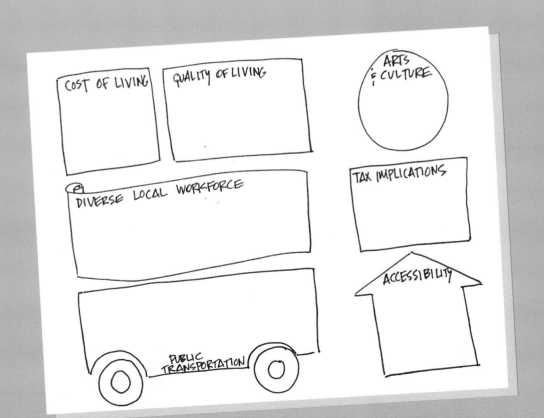

Teams are then assigned cities to research, mapping details onto this tool.

Apply the Pieces

Gameboarding begins with a brainstorm. Ideas on Post-its are attached to the appropriate block.

After exhausting the realm of possibility, whittle down entries. This is where stickies shine. Test solutions, moving them off, on, or around the board. Combine concepts when helpful by creating fresh, legible notes. Make difficult decisions about what matters most, and discard the rest.

Each field should present concepts in hierarchical importance.

Consider quantity, scope, and color of entries, allowing gameboards to go through multiple iterations. Reflect, share, collect feedback, and tweak until the strategy is both achievable and extraordinary.

How broad or narrow should a Post-it entry be?

Suppose you need to identify the audience(s) for a given project. Some GAMEs attempt to reach everyone, but that's preposterous. Human beings are not some monolithic mass. Trying to be all things to all people usually backfires, generating pedestrian compromises that aren't particularly enthralling to anyone.

Even "18–75 year old women" is awfully broad. Few people strongly self-identify as a female within this 57-year range. "Health care professionals," "doctors," and "podiatrists" feel progressively more connected to certain individuals, though the pool of candidates shrinks with added specificity.

Each note represents a project.

Ensure its scope makes sense.

Scope

Quantity

Completed blocks typically house 1–5 Post-its.

Shoot for as few as possible, yet as many as needed. Too many translates to an unmanageable plan. Too few signify trouble, with insufficient strategy to reach success.

Don't disguise five entries as one, but be careful not to torpedo efforts by pursuing too many disparate projects with competing needs.

Each entry requires unique resources.

Color

Small paper spans the rainbow.

Beyond adding variety and aesthetics, contrasting colors can signify various meanings. Think strategically, and create a *legend*. For example, perhaps the following colors indicate:

CONCEPT	Yellow	Green	Blue
PRIORITY	low	medium	high
GOAL	short-term	medium-term	long-term
EXPENSE	cheap	moderate	pricey
DIFFERENTIATION	traditional	variation	radical
CONTRIBUTION	Mary	Harry	Larry
SUPERVISES THIS ASPECT	Aaron	Karen	Sharon
GAMEBOARD CONNECTIONS	stream A	stream B	stream C

 A Board GAME

⭐ CHALLENGE: **Design a nontraditional concert that sells out.**

Art Promo is the marketing director for a regional orchestra. Though the group sounds great, their hall is at half capacity for most performances, and patrons are aging.

Leadership pressures Art to do better, but he suspects another problem.

What if performances simply aren't relevant?

No amount of PR can fix that!

To generate novel proposals, he designs a multiteam GAME. Played by musicians, staff, and board members, Art's *Arts Marketing A-list* forces holistic thinking about event design and promotion.

Multiple teams receive large poster-size gameboards highlighting six aspects:

A RT	What's the experience?
A UDIENCE	Who's the customer?
A LLIES	Which strategic partners?
A NGLE	How is buzz generated?
A LLURE	What incentivizes attendance?
A RSENAL	Which advertising tools?

Each field is further broken down to help guide the process.

After defining implications, Art explains that not every subcategory must ultimately include entries. Rather, this second-level detail is supplied to catalyze and organize strategy. Address only what is necessary.

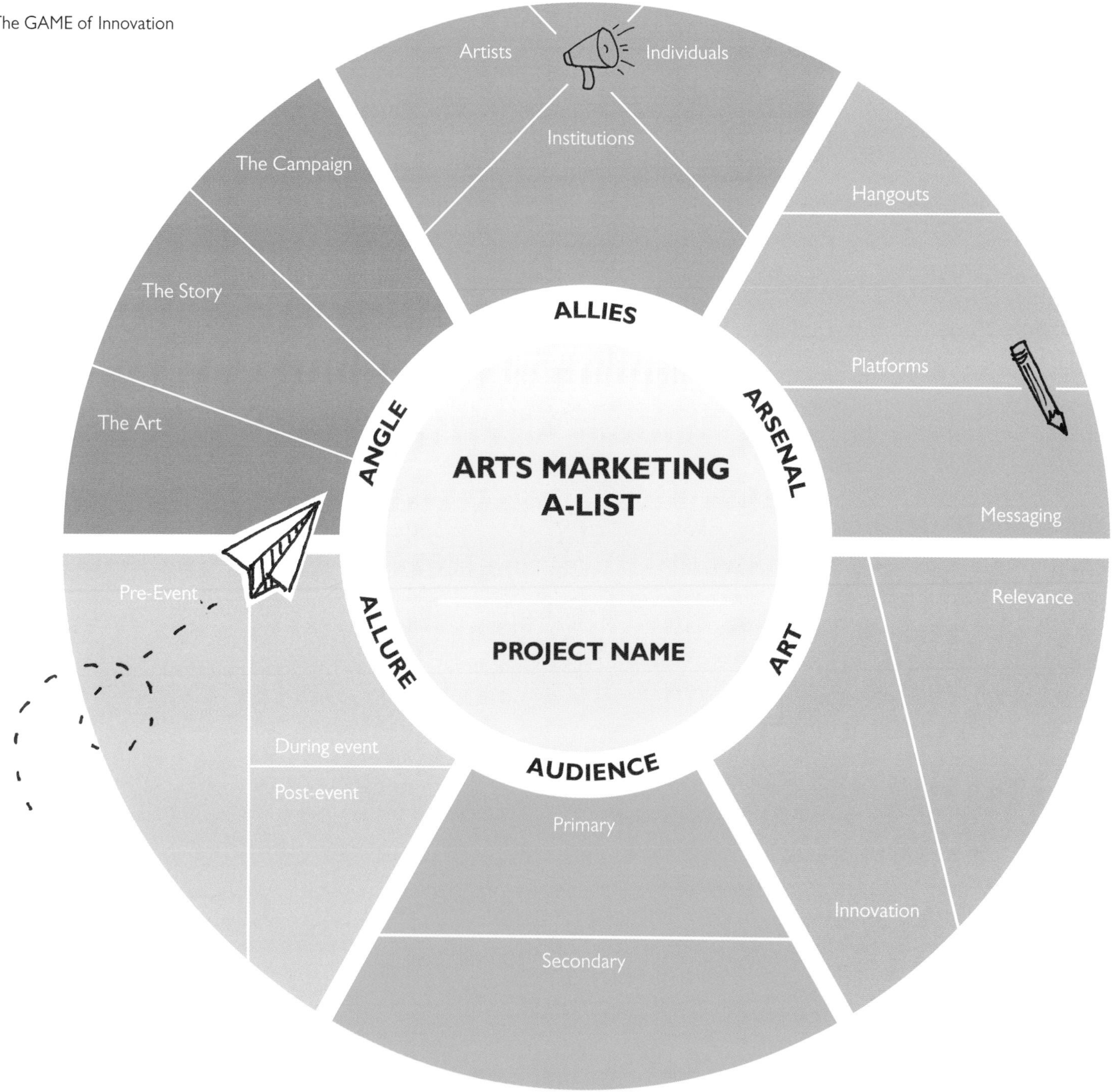

ALLIES

Artists
Individuals
Institutions

The Campaign

The Story

The Art

ANGLE

ARSENAL

Hangouts

Platforms

Messaging

Relevance

**ARTS MARKETING
A-LIST**

PROJECT NAME

ART

Innovation

Primary

Secondary

AUDIENCE

ALLURE

Pre-Event

During event

Post-event

Notating approaches on Post-its, puzzlers have five minutes to brainstorm and refine each block before moving on.

The order of fields is determined by rolling a die, ensuring a different sequence for each team.

Varying the progression leads to vastly different outcomes.

For example, consider how differently strategy might evolve if the first three fields were:

Sequence A

1. **Allies.** Who are great strategic partners?

2. **Audience.** Which people can they easily reach?

3. **Art.** What kind of event would that audience love?

Sequence B

1. **Allure.** What cool incentives would encourage folks to attend?

2. **Angle.** How might we make those incentives buzz-worthy dinnertime conversations?

3. **Audience.** Who will be compelled?

Sequence C

1. **Audience.** What nontraditional audiences should we target?

2. **Allure.** What will entice them to attend?

3. **Arsenal.** How can we reach them?

Sequence D

1. **Angle.** How might we create *huge* buzz?

2. **Allies.** Which partners will best amplify that message?

3. **Art.** What event features might emphasize our angle?

Identify
MATERIALS
most likely to capture ideas, ignite imagination, and build the remarkable.

CHAPTER **4**

EXPERIENCE

When building an EXPERIENCE, determine the
GAME type (**S**orts) and sequence of activities (**S**tructure).
This chapter concludes with several examples (**S**amples).

What process?

EXPERIENCE

A leader facing a serious challenge recognizes the need to take action. Perhaps it's time to eliminate inefficiencies, transform institutional culture, or reimagine an underperforming product that once was a hit.

After setting the stage, she takes the plunge. *"What should we do?"* I call it the:

ONE STOP FLOP.

Unfortunately, this process is likely doomed before it begins. Unless the challenge is particularly simple, discussions predictably spiral out of control. They leap erratically from topic to topic, achieving little more than calamity and frustration. Dissent barges in, blocking any chance of progress. Or puzzlers line up behind obvious, yet wholly insufficient, conclusions.

Truth be told, the one-stop flop isn't a process at all. It's simply shooting blindfolded. Discovering innovation with an uninspired, isolated question is improbable at best.

Given **G**UIDELINES and **A**RENA, innovation champions integrate a number of **M**ATERIALS when designing meticulously crafted **E**XPERIENCES.

They architect an approach (**S**orts) and series of activities (**S**tructure) likely to catalyze the remarkable. Journeys (**S**amples) are mapped strategically, yet creative solutions are never prescribed.

Great GAMEs maximize the chance of a win, while giving power to the puzzlers.

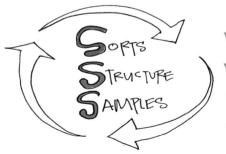

What GAME type?

What happens?

What are some examples?

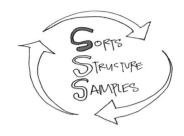

Sorts
Structure
Samples

SORTS

What GAME type?

What kind of Experience will you design? Does it simply advance through a series of questions or pursue a less conventional approach? Will there be one or multiple teams? Is it competitive or collaborative? GAME formats are virtually endless. In addition to the following genres, find inspiration in game store aisles and "reality" shows.

1. Solitaire

Most puzzling techniques are directly applicable to individuals. But there are challenges. Soloists invite just one perspective. Trickier yet, they tend to dive in without a formal process. Working alone, it is more—not less—important to impose clear guidelines, process, and ground rules. Build the road map first, solve later. Better yet, have someone else play or design your GAME.

Example: Page 145

2. Single Team Play

With just one team, everyone rows in the same direction (when it counts). Your sole opponent is the problem itself. Can it be beat? Though larger groups may be subdivided at times, be careful not to dilute efforts with competing priorities. Stay focused on earning that big prize.

Example: Page 141

MY IDEA

3. Tournaments

Friendly competition among multiple teams encourages puzzlers to invest energy and dream big. After battling proposals are pitched, organization leaders, external judges, or an audience votes to select the winner(s).

Example: Page 136

4. Fusion Rounds

Following independent teamwork, the best elements of multiple proposals are combined. Equitable representation is not the assumed goal. Rather, arrive at powerful, blended solutions. The process of synthesis can be navigated by an entire community or external council with fresh eyes.

Example: Page 139

6. Point Systems

Achievement-based incentives like points or badges, a staple of video games, stress the relative importance of benchmarks. These embedded clues suggest where energy might be placed. Some systems involve fixed awards—do this, earn X. Others clarify maximum point counts, with actual scores based on quality. While quantifiable encouragement pushes some to work harder, those who fall behind sometimes lose motivation.

Example: Page 143

5. Board Games

Gameboards help develop strategies for mapping interconnected priorities. This tool can be incorporated throughout a GAME Experience or limited to certain phases. Puzzlers are often free to navigate fields as the muse strikes. Alternatively, the sequence may be prescribed, consequential if conclusions *here* impact decisions *there*. Altering a process can change the outcome.

Example: Page 115

7. Role-Play

Stepping into someone else's shoes builds empathy. Provided with a profile and plot, puzzlers must act, think, and make decisions from their character's perspective. This format provides an opportunity to test reactions or compare tactics side by side.

Example: Page 144

8. Card GAMEs

Concept cards are used to determine process, constraints, resources, and more. Cards can be shuffled and dealt, pulled from a deck, chosen from a display, drawn from a hat, or discovered through a scavenger hunt.

Example: Page 106

10. Obstacle Courses

One mini-challenge (game-within-a-GAME) must be completed before progressing to the next. Speed is prioritized, but moving too quickly causes strategic blunders. While the notion of an obstacle course is effective metaphorically, it is energizing when teams literally advance to different physical environments.

Example: When imagining a new product, a boutique soap-making company challenges multiple teams to solve a series of interrelated puzzles before moving on to the next. This progressive format encourages puzzlers to work quickly. Stations focus on: (1) scent, (2) ingredients, (3) appearance, (4) storytelling, (5) packaging, (6) labeling. Each team emerges with a comprehensive strategy.

9. Elimination Contests

Survival of the fittest . . . At various points, puzzlers are "kicked off the island" through competition or votes. One possibility is dismissal, shrinking the population until a champion emerges. Another variation requires losing teams to join forces with prevailing ones until a single community stands united.

Example: 16 designers are charged with conceiving a groundbreaking roller coaster. After each round, judges hear pairs of proposals (A vs. B, C vs. D, etc.), choosing the best of each to advance to the next phase. Losing teams join forces with their winning counterparts, developing that concept further.

ROUND 1 *16 teams of 1* **basic concept**	ROUND 2 *8 teams of 2* **details & WOWables**
ROUND 3 *4 teams of 4* **2D drawing**	ROUND 4 *2 teams of 8* **3D prototyping**

For the final round, all 16 puzzlers improve the victorious vision, unified as a community.

STRUCTURE

What happens?

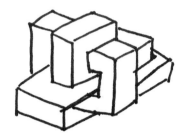

Building the optimal Experience is a puzzle in itself. What happens, in which order, for how long? Numerous variables must be considered:

- Nature of challenge
- Puzzlers involved
- Time period allocated
- Experiential priorities

Multiple approaches are always possible, though not all will be equivalent.

There is no officially sanctioned, one-size-fits-all formula.

Like great stories, the best examples are curated adventures with a distinct beginning, middle, and end. This is true whether puzzling lasts a month, day, or hour. A typical skeleton follows.

Openings are crucial, setting a tone for the entire Experience.

beginning
STUDY

Common activities/phases:

⟹ Examine challenge   ⟹ Define insights/design principles

⟹ Hunt for clues   ⟹ Reframe the challenge

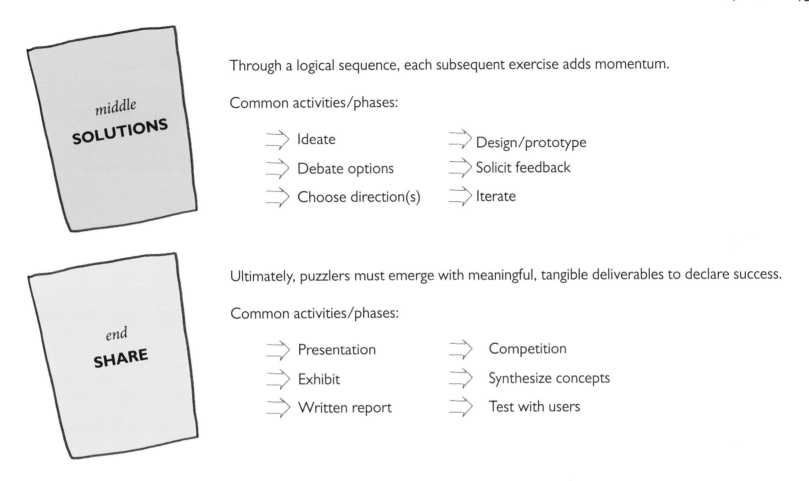

Through a logical sequence, each subsequent exercise adds momentum.

Common activities/phases:

⇒ Ideate		⇒ Design/prototype
⇒ Debate options		⇒ Solicit feedback
⇒ Choose direction(s)		⇒ Iterate

Ultimately, puzzlers must emerge with meaningful, tangible deliverables to declare success.

Common activities/phases:

⇒ Presentation		⇒ Competition
⇒ Exhibit		⇒ Synthesize concepts
⇒ Written report		⇒ Test with users

As you design an Experience,

Consider both PRODUCT and PROCESS.

Beyond generating spectacularly innovative solutions, great GAMEs should strengthen the team. Be sensitive to emotional trajectories bound to arise. Players are generally positive early on, but stress can build over time.

In the end, communities should feel proud of their efforts, rallying behind a sense of collective purpose.

Define Large-Scale "Phases" First

When designing an innovation Experience, start with the big picture and zoom in gradually.

What major puzzle pieces will shape your GAME?

Begin by determining large-scale *phases*. Like chapters in a book, the title, duration, and scope of each is up to its author.

As you brainstorm, notate concepts on small paper (Post-its or index cards), to be organized, categorized, rearranged, or eliminated later. Capture phase titles with concise, one- to three-word labels that clearly identify the central objective. Examples include:

Though there is no correct quantity, the optimal number is influenced by the nature of a challenge, total time period, duration per phase, and what is necessary to reach your goal.

A typical Experience contains:

Overall Period	# of Phases
Short GAME (30 minutes to 2 hours)	2–3
Medium GAME (half to full day)	3–6
Long GAME (2 days or more)	5–8+

Map the Structure

There are several approaches to mapping the structure of an innovation GAME.

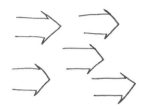

Work FORWARD

Determine a logical opener, move to phase 2,
phase 3, and so on until the process is complete.

Work BACKWARD

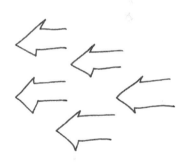

Start from the end, planning in reverse chronology.

Work INWARD

If beginning and end are apparent, but the middle is
fuzzy, connect dots accordingly.

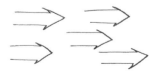 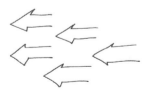

Adjust sequencing until the big pieces interlock. Each phase should add value and momentum, leading logically to the next. Omit what is extraneous. Tweak until your Experience outline feels strong from top to bottom.

Summarize the "PLOT"

PHASE — *Which chapter? (#)*

LABEL — *What title? (1–2 words)*

OVERVIEW — *What happens? (1–2 sentences)*

TIME — *How long? (duration or clock)*

Continuing the storytelling metaphor, you now have a table of contents. Provide additional details when scripting the PLOT, or experiential overview.

Below is a basic PLOT based on Stanford University's renowned approach to *Design Thinking*. Three sets of timings are included, demonstrating possibilities for short (90-minute), medium (4-hour with break), and long (5-day) GAMEs.

Phase	**L**abel	**O**verview	**T**ime		
			short	*medium*	*long*
1	EMPATHIZE	Plan for and interview subjects to discover ELATION/FANTASY/PAIN points.	20 min	50 min	Day 1
2	DEFINE	Transform INSIGHTS into design principles that reframe the problem.	15 min	30 min	Day 2 (9–1)
3	IDEATE	Brainstorm SOLUTIONS, debate options, choose a direction.	20 min	45 min	Days 2 (1–6) & 3
4	PROTOTYPE	Build a MODEL that clarifies details and design.	20 min	1 hour	Day 4
5	TEST	Share with potential users for FEEDBACK.	15 min	40 min	Day 5

Detail Your "PLANS"

After determining large-scale phases, break them down further into steps. For example:

Phase 1—INTERVIEW

Step A: discuss goals

Step B: write questions

Step C: assign roles

Step D: conduct interview

Phase 2—FRAMING

Step A: analyze interview

Step B: isolate key takeaways

Step C: identify insights

Step D: choose design principle(s)

Step E: reframe challenge

Phase 3—IDEATION

Step A: general brainstorm

Step B: concept card brainstorm

. . . and so forth

Several parameters define each step. Clarify by detailing your PLANS (discussed over the next several pages. For sample PLANS, see page 142).

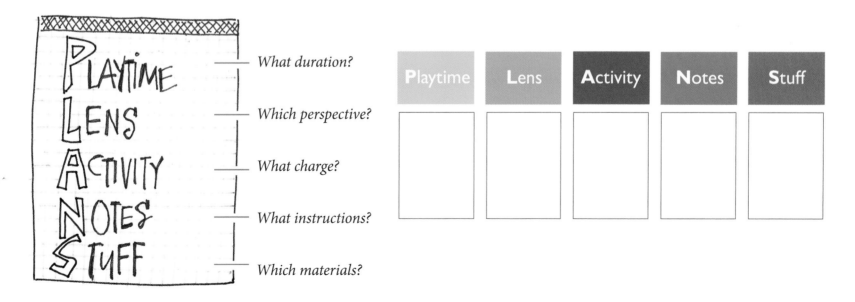

PLAYTIME —— *What duration?*

LENS —— *Which perspective?*

ACTIVITY —— *What charge?*

NOTES —— *What instructions?*

STUFF —— *Which materials?*

Playtime	Lens	Activity	Notes	Stuff

PLAYTIME:
What duration?

One of the most challenging aspects of problem solving is time management. In good GAMEs, the minutes fly by. In bad ones, they drag on eternally. Progress is most likely with clear structures . . . and not quite enough time. Assigning strict limits helps participants plan accordingly, while adding urgency.

Nothing gets done without a deadline.

Predicting the duration necessary for various activities is a skill that gets better with experience. Skimping translates to sloppy work or incomplete tasks. Lavishing imperils the finish line. The trick is identifying just the right amount of time.

In the Playtime column, write either (a) allocated minutes or (b) projected start time. Suppose you are planning a 50-minute phase for a given process. The breakdown might look as follows:

Phase 1 (50 minutes)	Start Time	Duration
Overview	3:00	5 min
Step A	3:05	12 min
Step B	3:17	7 min
Step C	3:24	15 min
Step D	3:39	4 min
Buffer	3:43	(7min)
End	3:50	

Note that just 43 minutes have been scheduled despite a slightly wider window. Such cushions permit flexibility. Each activity requires at least some explanation, and things often take longer than anticipated. Somebody will need to have directions repeated. The projector will malfunction. The time allocation will prove insufficient. Don't let unexpected hiccups defeat your effort.

Always leave buffers.

"There's nothing an artist needs more—even excellent tools or stamina—than a deadline."

—Adriana Trigiani, American fiction author

LENS:
Which perspective?

Every activity should clearly imply a single perspective, or Lens (the focus of Chapters 5–9). Each of five outlooks is invoked by a color and a term starting with the same letter.

G	Green	Gather
B	Blue	Boost
O	Orange	Own
P	Purple	Propose
R	Red	Rip

ACTIVITY:
What charge?

Each step involves exactly one Activity. Make descriptions concise, compelling, and easy to understand. The challenge for puzzlers should be generating quality results, not comprehending instructions.

Activities can be presented as QUESTIONS:

• What do we know about existing customers?
• If we had an unlimited budget, what would we do?
• Which solutions are innovative yet realistic?
• What do you love about these options?
• What could go wrong?

Or actionable COMMANDS:

• Conduct interview
• Brainstorm solutions
• Share, cluster, study
• Offer praise
• Critique proposals
• Choose favorite

NOTES:
What instructions?

Add pertinent details not indicated elsewhere. For example:

- Does the activity require further clarification?
- Will puzzlers sit or stand?
- Do they work in a secondary space?
- What else should be communicated?

Notes commonly indicate changing MODEs of engagement. In other words:

For this activity, how will puzzlers function?

Team	Everyone has the same "job" in a "flat" organization.
Chamber	Temporarily divided into "subcommittees."
Solo	Puzzlers work individually.
Roles	Specific responsibilities are designated. *e.g., interviewer, scribe, doodler, timer, observer, perspective advocate*
Cameo	One or more guest contributors participate. *e.g., interview subject, guest presenter, judge*

STUFF:
Which materials?

Finally, identify which Stuff (physical materials, Chapter 3) best enhances each step. This may include:

GATHERABLES
- Writing implements (e.g., pens, pencils, crayons)
- Small paper (Post-its, note cards)
- Large surfaces (flip charts, whiteboards)
- Adhesives (glues, tapes)
- Prototyping supplies (anything you've got)
- Technology (laptops, cameras, projectors)

GEAR
Specialty GAME items like handouts, concept cards, dice, timers, currency, bingo drums, spinners, and so on.

GAMEBOARDS
Any kind of mapping tool.

Variety keeps the process interesting.

Multiteam Variations

As counterintuitive as it sounds, imaginations invited to run wild arrive at surprisingly few destinations. I frequently witness teams brimming with excitement about their novel proposal, only to discover that two other groups designed near replicas. When multiple groups develop similar ideas:

It's either an epic winner—or fairly obvious . . .

To minimize redundancy, consider the process.

Identical Process	**Contrasting Variables**	**Reshuffled Process**
The simplest solution is keeping things consistent and hoping that groups naturally discover divergent paths.	Present teams with dissimilar variables, such as:	The same activities in an altered order can trigger vastly different outcomes.
This approach may indeed work, particularly when teams have deliberately unique makeups: different ages, sectors, religions, worldviews, and so on.	• Challenges (Chapter1) • Constraints (Chapter 1) • Avatars (Chapter 3) For example, suppose a Team A Constraint requires spending less than $100; Team B should disperse $5,000–10,000; Team C may allocate no less than $1 million. Divergent thought is almost inevitable.	For example, one team might begin with interviews before committing to design principles. Another could identify desirable outcomes first and then solicit feedback through interviews.
That said, puzzlers regularly gravitate toward similar magnetic concepts. To increase the likelihood of variety, build GAME processes to curtail the risk of duplication.	Another possibility is imposing varied conditions along the way. Perhaps competitors draw unique concepts from a deck. Because no two cards are the same, variety is guaranteed.	Sequence matters. Each activity influences subsequent ones. Altering the order profoundly changes an Experience and even the ultimate solution.

The Opportunity of Interludes

During innovation GAMEs, most of the action consists of *TeamTime*. Puzzlers are challenged to work actively and collaboratively as they tackle meaningful PLANS embedded in the process.

For extended Experiences, consider pausing play (as appropriate) to allow for interludes. The best options add variety, strategy, and clues, while strengthening community. My events often incorporate activities we call:

OVERTURES	Short keynotes or other presentations (30 minutes max).
PUZZLER-U	Facilitated classes related to assignments, where attendees learn concepts, strategize, and workshop ideas. With large groups, members from each team are divided among multiple offerings, depending upon their role.
HUDDLES	Interactive strategy sessions on becoming a better puzzler, not directly related to the GAME. For example, we might focus on using Great Gaming Goggles (Chapter 5), cultivating creativity (Chapter 7), or addressing prickly personalities (Chapter 11).
DANZES	Art-making workshops emphasizing transferable lessons (drawing to teach visual communication; miming to teach nonverbal communication, tango dancing to teach leadership, drumming to teach collaboration perspectives, etc.).
BIG IDEAS	Prepared TED-talk-like sessions featuring participating puzzlers (maximum: 10 minutes each) around innovative approaches.
ENTREPRETAINMENT	More than entertainment, performances are somehow tied to the GAME.
MEALTIME	Typically 30 to 90 minutes, allows folks to rejuvenate and socialize. When time is in short supply, working meals challenge teams to simultaneously address prompts.

SAMPLES

What are some examples?

The remainder of this chapter outlines a diversity of innovation GAMEs, demonstrating how they might be conceptualized.

Please note, attention is placed on experience design rather than solutions generated (addressed in Parts B and C of this book).

CHALLENGE: What WOW innovations might save us?

Toy Store-EEE is a small retail chain that sells playthings to "children of all ages." Like so many brick-and-mortar vendors, their survival is threatened by proliferating competition on- and off-line.

Determined to stay relevant and sustainable, manager Mary Times recognizes the urgent need to evolve their business model, perhaps radically.

In order to generate bold proposals while bolstering a culture of innovation, she conceives a trio of Experiences to be played by different groups of employees. While all address the same large-scale objective, note how each is built around a unique framing challenge.

Long GAME: *"Fun Palace"*

ARENA

Period: 2 days (9 a.m. to 6 p.m.)

Puzzlers: 50 employees (8 teams of 6–7)

Place: Warehouse in a shopping district, with common space plus team rooms

Toys are synonymous with "fun." But most emporiums are fairly sterile, even stressful places. This human-centered tournament, modeled after the classic design thinking approach described on page 128, challenges puzzlers to transform traditional box stores into enticing destinations.

★ **CHALLENGE: How might our toy store become an in-demand FUN PALACE?**

This GAME's PLOT (Phase, Label, Overview, Time) is shared over the next two pages.

Give Me a Break!

As a rule of thumb, 10- to 15-minute breaks (I call them TimeOuts) should be scheduled at least once every two hours. Allow puzzlers to use the facilities, check email, and rest their cerebrums. For online experiences, shorter 5-minute pauses may suffice.

Note: Breaks are omitted from the following PLOT, but incorporated in real time.

DAY 1

INTRO	**Overview/Basics**	**9:00**
	Introduction, overview, Guidelines. Quick icebreaker, name team, create team poster, elect captain, assign rooms.	9:00 9:15
Phase 1	**Empathy**	**9:45**
	Visiting schools, playgrounds, parks, and businesses, use observations/interviews to study FUN. *What do folks love? What would they love? What can't they love?*	
LUNCH		**12:45**
Phase 2	**Define**	**1:30**
	Reflect on research. Discuss empathy points. Identify key insights. Reframe the Challenge.	
Phase 3	**Ideation**	**3:00**
	Brainstorm solutions, debate proposals, choose a BIG idea to develop.	
Phase 4	**Details/Storyboarding**	**4:30**
	Work through specifics and determine "WOWables." Storyboard the proposed user experience.	
DAY END	**Happy Hour** (optional)	**6:00**

DAY 2

Phase 5	**Review/Development**	**9:00**
	Discuss yesterday's conclusions. Fix up storyboard and prepare simple overview.	
Phase 6	**Consultancy**	**10:00**
	Local experts meet with teams to offer feedback on storyboard and proposal.	
Phase 7	**Prototyping/Pitch Prep**	**11:00**
	Incorporate critique, as appropriate. Subdivide teams to build a prototype and prepare a pitch. Take lunch break between 12:00–1:30 (as you wish). Presentation slides due by 3:15.	
Phase 8	**Reveal** (Competition)	**4:00**
	Each team pitches for 3 minutes, followed by 3 minutes of Q & A with judges.	4:00
	Audience votes and judges deliberate.	5:00
	Entire community reflects on the Experience. Judge and Audience Choice Awards announced.	5:15
EVENT END	**Home to Sleep!** (Zzz . . .)	**6:00**

Medium GAME: *"Come In!"*

ARENA

INTRO	**Overview**	9:00
Phase I	**Avatars**	9:10

Period: 3 hours (9 a.m. to noon)

Puzzlers: 25 employees (5 teams of 5), led by a GAME master

Place: Auditorium in local library

Each team is provided with two-thirds of an avatar BIO (<u>B</u>ackground and <u>I</u>mage) and then challenged to complete the profile.

Brick-and-mortar stores have at least three major disadvantages when compared to online competitors: (1) less inventory, (2) more overhead (resulting in higher prices), and (3) customer inconvenience. Therefore, vendors that simply sell things find themselves in an untenable situation. This GAME seeks to explore potential benefits that physical locations might have over virtual ones.

What is this target customer's <u>O</u>utlook? Which interests, hobbies, and motivators do they have? What are turnoffs?

CHALLENGE: **What unique, compelling rationale will deliver customers to our door?**

This GAME's PLOT is written differently to illustrate the flexibility of this planning approach.

| Phase 2 | **Motivators** | 9:30 |

Teams brainstorm: "What innovations might excite our avatar to visit the store longer or more often?" (10 minutes). They then have 3 minutes apiece to consider five *What If?* questions, dealt from a deck of concept cards. By phase end, each table should look like a shaggy Post-it carpet.

| Phase 3 | **Debate/Decide** | 10:00 |

Teams nominate promising concepts, discuss pros/cons, choose one.

BREAK

| Phase 4 | **Poster Creation** | 10:45 |

Work out important features. Produce compelling visual document with pertinent details.

| Phase 5 | **Share & Blend** | 11:20 |

Present concepts to full community, 2 minutes per team, while sharing posters. Then discuss ways to fuse promising aspects of various proposals.

EVENT END   12:00

The End

 # Short GAME: *"Tech Revolution"*

 **ARENA**

Period: 60 minutes

Puzzlers: 8 employees (single team) plus facilitator

Place: Board room

To instigate radical thinking, suspend pragmatism and conventional wisdom (at least temporarily).

But that's tricky when worldviews are overwhelmed by "the way things are." Peering into the future makes it easier to consider alternate realities.

In this GAME, Mary transports puzzlers 15 years down the road. After imagining breakthrough inventions that reshape the toy store experience, they return to the present, picturing innovations that might be implemented today.

★ **CHALLENGE: How might breakthrough technology transform our business model?**

For this short GAME, complete step-by-step PLANS (Playtime, Lens, Activity, Notes, Stuff) are shown.

Playtime	Lens	Activity	Notes	Stuff
3 min.		Welcome/GAME Overview	sit at single table	–
6 min.	P	What breakthrough technologies might be available in 15 years?	Goal: MANY entries! 4-word max each e.g., "talking robots"	Index cards
3 min.	O	Small groups choose ONE concept each	MODE: Divide into 4 duos	Take selected index card
10 min.	P	DEVELOP remarkable future initiative where concept shapes toy store experience	4 duos around room, jot down details, title your program	Flip charts attached to walls
4 min.	G	PITCH concepts to room	1 min max per duo, present from wall	Verbal, may refer to flip chart
6 min.	B	What did you LIKE about presented concepts?	Return to table, only positive affirmations	Discussion only
5 min.	O	VOTE and choose favorite	Placed on flip charts, assign 2 votes to same or different projects	2 stickers/person
10 min.	P	Reimagine concept to be implemented NOW	Single scribe, facilitated discussion	Whiteboard
5 min.	P	Next steps (How might we take this idea further?)	Discussion, single notetaker	Laptop

52 min. + buffer

Now that we've examined three approaches to a single challenge, consider additional scenarios.

Point System: *"Sister Act"*

Kirbyville is thrilled about the adoption of their sister city, Coleslawvakia.

 CHALLENGE: What meaningful, buzz-worthy initiative should link our communities?

Twelve diverse teams engage in an immersive, weeklong tournament. Ultimately, an impressive $250,000 will be dispersed to multiple projects. Better yet, the top team receives an all-expense paid visit. While judges make the final call, some thirty achievements increase a team's score, including:

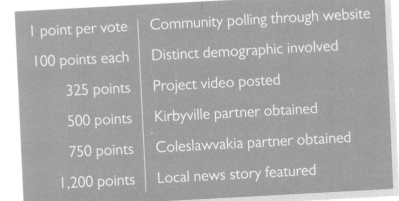

1 point per vote	Community polling through website
100 points each	Distinct demographic involved
325 points	Project video posted
500 points	Kirbyville partner obtained
750 points	Coleslawvakia partner obtained
1,200 points	Local news story featured

This point system helps teams strategize about where to focus energy. It also adds competitive excitement, while energizing populations from both communities.

Role-Play: *"Bridge the Gap"*

A colossal gap between the "haves" and "have nots" of Gulf Town is undeniable. As inequality grows, fiercely different ideas about community priorities have led to hostility, distrust, and gridlock.

To generate solutions while better grasping realities, city manager Derek Torr arranges a role-playing GAME. Twelve local leaders representing various perspectives become "lead actors."

 CHALLENGE: Build consensus around addressing our equity gap.

The plot takes place in a fictional town reminiscent of Gulf Town, and characters resemble several profiles in the room. But rather than playing familiar perspectives, roles are assigned randomly. As a result, several puzzlers assume identities of individuals not at all like them. In fact, a few people are initially upset after discovering they must represent "the adversary."

Participants are given reading materials describing the scenario and their designated character's profile. During meetings, an improvised play

unfolds. As conflict emerges, the GAME master works to build empathy and harmony.

This process unearths several promising proposals, but that's not the only benefit. Several actors begin identifying emotionally with their character, developing a deeper appreciation for good people on all sides of this issue.

Puzzlers are transformed.

Solitaire: *"Sermon Shakeup"*

Pastor Claire G. Mann has a reputation for delivering inspiring, varied preaching. But lately, she's fallen into a rut and is short on creative ideas.

To stimulate new ways of thinking, Claire asks Rabbi Haas Idik to design a solitaire GAME for her to play. His approach, inspired by word games, is simple but effective. Each instruction is sealed in a separate numbered envelope, not to be opened until the previous step has been completed.

★ **CHALLENGE: Script an unusually noteworthy sermon.**

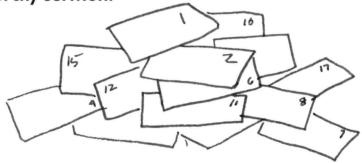

GAME instructions:

1. Choose general sermon TOPIC.
2. Pick 2 LETTERS at random from a bingo drum (e.g., D and P).
3. Brainstorm & number 6 HISTORICAL FIGURES, real or fictional, beginning with 1st letter (Darwin, Da Vinci, Donald Duck, etc.).
4. Roll a die (1–6), and select corresponding entry. Sermon should demonstrate how this character relates to overriding topic.
5. Brainstorm & number 6 ACTIVITIES beginning with 2nd letter (Piano, Painting, Pineapple carving, etc.).
6. Roll die again (1–6), and select corresponding entry. Sermon should somehow involve this activity, perhaps literally onstage. Collaboration encouraged!
7. Call me and share results!

■ **The key** to solving complex, creative challenges?

Design powerhouse **EXPERIENCES**, destined to catalyze success.

COLOR YOUR PERSPECTIVE

Align thinking with the
five lenses of innovation.

COLOR YOUR PERSPECTIVE

Part B Overview

Part A explored a framework for building innovation GAMEs. Now it's time to color the specifics.

Design activities likely to catalyze breakthrough invention.

Each challenge is different, and many tools are available. Part B unveils a range of approaches I integrate into my own GAMEs and recommend to clients. As with earlier chapters, contextualized scenarios demonstrate principles in action. To illustrate how they might play out, potential solutions are often presented.

Chapter 6

Puzzlers must become master detectives. Using the GREEN/GATHER lens, hunt for clues, LEARN about crucial aspects (**L**ogistics, **E**motions, **A**ssumptions, **R**esources, **N**arrative), and interpret valuable data.

Chapter 7

Innovation requires imagination. Using the PURPLE/PROPOSE lens, remember seven brainstorming rules, apply these 10 creative catalysts, and prototype your vision.

Chapter 8

Both BLUE/BOOST (positive) and RED/RIP (negative) feedback are critical for innovation. Weighing the psychological implications of these lenses, this chapter offers six critiquing techniques.

Chapter 5

IMPROVE YOUR VISION with the five lenses of innovation. GAMEs and teams should align thinking modes during each step of the process.

Chapter 9

Puzzlers switch on the ORANGE/OWN lens when making decisions. After considering why it's so difficult to choose, this chapter introduces nine techniques for committing to one direction at the expense of many others.

CHAPTER **5**

IMPROVE YOUR VISION

IMPROVE YOUR VISION with the five lenses of innovation.
GAMEs and teams should align thinking modes
during each step of the process.

What perspective?

IMPROVE YOUR VISION

Suppose your team brainstorms.

Suggestions start to fly. Momentum builds—until someone disparages, "That's a terrible idea." Another puzzler offers a history lesson: "We tried that 10 years ago."

Make no mistake. Critical feedback is, well, critical. So is historical reflection. Just not during ideation.

Even if comments are 100 percent accurate, now simply isn't the time. Beyond stealing valuable seconds, it poisons the air. In the future, explorers may become hesitant to contribute. Why stick out my neck, just to be shot down?

The human mind is capable of a great many things. It can imagine, recall, interpret, critique, praise, ponder, and commit. Incoming data is channeled to your head (analysis) or heart (emotion). A logical left-brain is married to a creative right-brain counterpart.

Innovation champions skillfully tap into all these aptitudes. However, they avoid the urge to access competing perspectives simultaneously.

Cognitive multitasking is horribly inefficient.

Problem Solving Blindfolded

A Puzzler Company Drama

Part comedy, part drama, part tragedy, the play that follows features five colleagues challenged to solve an important puzzle. Though characters are fictional, countless real-life meetings inspired this work.

Character List

3

Rip D'Schredz

Lives up to his name. Disparages everything. Takes no prisoners.

1

Dee Cydes

Runs the show (or tries to). She just wants to make a choice. Any choice.

4

Gladys Hafful

Sees the good in any idea or situation. She's annoying in a sweet way.

2

Reid Surcher

A research geek. Never met a situation he didn't investigate.

5

Ivan Idear

Extremely creative, always full of solutions. His brain runs far and wild.

Dee Cydes (matter of fact)   You all know why I've called this meeting. Before we get going, are there opening remarks?

Reid Surcher (curious)   This is an interesting room. My analysis finds just 49 spaces with comparable dimensions in the entire state! Did you know the architect was born in Milan and raised by his nanny's grandmother's neighbor's friend?

Anyhoo, at the last meeting you mentioned the possibility of getting a whiteboard. I did research and created a spreadsheet. It's amazing what they make nowadays. One brand literally doubles as a cutting board!

Rip D'Schredz (suspicious)   That's a terrible idea!

Gladys Hafful (hopeful)   It does make sense to purchase multiuse items.

Ivan Idear (excited)   I LOVE combining concepts. Ohhh . . . here's an idea! How about a tattoo parlor for senior citizens? We could call it "Wrinkled Ink." What do you think? Hey, that rhymes!

Dee Cydes (reining things in)   Um, hang on. We're here to discuss this year's Magical Music Box fundraiser. Let's settle on a clear plan that raises $15,000. Did you get the agenda?

Reid Surcher	I did. I also conducted a quick online search and feel our goal may be off. Local organizations have raised more. *Amalgamated Mutton Chops* recently brought in $32,749. In a single night!
Rip D'Schredz	I must have you blocked as spam. No offense. Why do we even use email? Can't we find a different way to communicate? Especially since we share the same office?!?!
Gladys Hafful	Well, it is the best method for keeping running records. For example, we can easily search communications from last year's fundraiser.
Ivan Idear	Hey, since we all love karaoke, what if we communicated musically? We could turn meetings into sort of a musical revue each week! And then we could sell tickets, broadening our audience and providing new sources of revenue. Each show could start with an "Agenda Sing-Along," kind of like a Gilbert and Sullivan patter song. And then I could do an interpretive dance. Does anyone here juggle? Do magic?
Rip D'Schredz (passive aggressive)	If I could do magic, you would have vanished by now. TA-DA!
Dee Cydes	*Let's focus and recap last year's event.* We can incorporate successful parts and steer clear of obstacles. We did raise 12 grand, meaning a lot was done right. Can we use that as a framework?

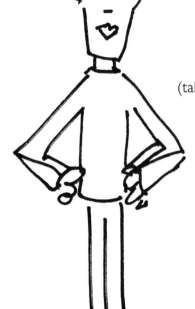

Rip D'Schredz (frustrated)

What's the point of looking back? That was then, this is now. So far after the fact, I'm not sure we can pinpoint specific things that did or didn't work.

Reid Surcher
(astonishingly nerdy)

Remember, production costs were 8.2 percent higher than predicted. While attendance was up by 6.2 percent, the overall amount per donor dropped by approximately 13.7928451 percent. We should also consider our donor base. I examined comps and discovered really interesting stats.

Gladys Hafful

I liked the idea of inviting well-heeled folks, grooming some to join our board.

Ivan Idear
(talking quickly and excitedly)

Last year's Magical Music Box Moonbounce was AWESOME!!! This time, we could have a big inflatable box that shoots out ping-pong balls with numbers on them, entering you into a drawing for extra minutes in the silent auction.

. . . Speaking of *silent* auctions . . . What if we had a mime handle it this year? Actually, she could be inside an "invisible" Magical Music Box! That would save money, since we wouldn't have to build anything. Or is that idea too inside the box? Ooooooh! Box lunches for meals! While watching a boxing match!! And everyone could get matching boxcars and a box of matches!!!!

Rip D'Schredz

There'd better be plenty of boxed wine.

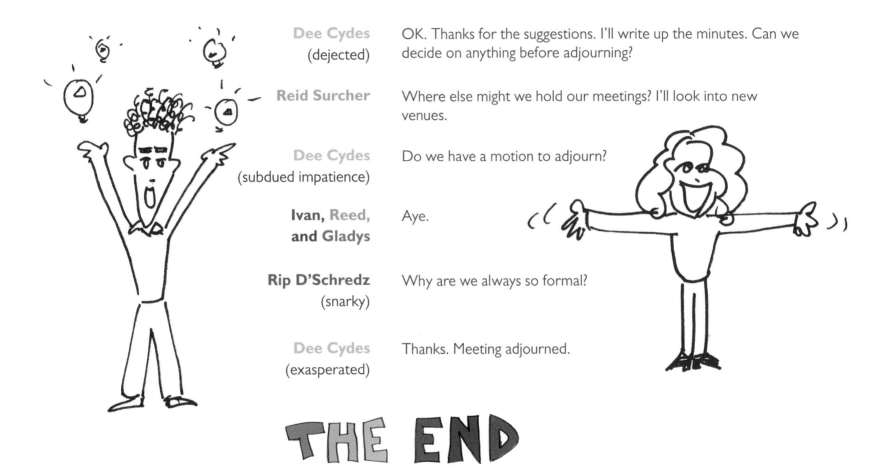

Dee Cydes (dejected)	OK. Thanks for the suggestions. I'll write up the minutes. Can we decide on anything before adjourning?
Reid Surcher	Where else might we hold our meetings? I'll look into new venues.
Dee Cydes (subdued impatience)	Do we have a motion to adjourn?
Ivan, Reed, and Gladys	Aye.
Rip D'Schredz (snarky)	Why are we always so formal?
Dee Cydes (exasperated)	Thanks. Meeting adjourned.

THE END

Have you ever witnessed a meeting that eerily resembled this one? For that matter, can you recall many that didn't?

Though meant to be comical, this play underscores serious challenges that afflict all but the most effective teams.

Great Gaming Goggles

Revolutionizing the art of innovation, Great Gaming Goggles (G³) are a breakthrough invention available everywhere imaginations are found. Easy to master, they quickly transform puzzling—when worn faithfully—improving efficiency and effectiveness.

G³ include five different colored lenses.

Furthermore, each color imposes a distinct perspective beginning with the same letter. All are powerful, and all may be necessary for cracking a particular puzzle. But there's a catch:

Just one lens type at a time.

Though widely divergent contributions are encouraged, G³ focus the brain, requiring puzzlers to stay in a single problem-solving lane. Combining two or more causes vision to get blurry.

On teams, G³ are controlled by a facilitator who simultaneously switches every puzzler's device to the same color. As a result, puzzlers work harmoniously and amplify progress.

Appropriate lenses should be baked into the GAME, supported with carefully worded prompts.

Though G³ are metaphorical, it can be helpful to reinforce implications with physical items. When training communities to use this tool, *The Puzzler Company* often incorporates cutout paper colored frames, on sticks.

"Multitasking divides your attention and leads to confusion and weakened focus."

—Deepak Chopra, Indian American writer and alternative medicine advocate

The 5 Lenses of Innovation

Techniques for maximizing the power of each lens are described in a corresponding chapter.

Green / **G**ather	**What can be learned?**	*research and analyze*	Chapter 6	
Purple / **P**ropose	**What can be imagined?**	*generate creative ideas or content*	Chapter 7	
Blue / **B**oost	**What works?**	*elevate, offer positive support*	Chapter 8	
Red / **R**ip	**What's wrong?**	*anticipate problems, pose constructive critique*	Chapter 8	
Orange / **O**wn	**What decision?**	*make a choice, commit*	Chapter 9	

Character Breakdown

Characters from *Problem Solving Blindfolded* may be hardworking and well-intentioned. But they need help with puzzling. Each colleague is limited to a single perspective, causing friction at every turn.

Like these puzzlers, most people are intuitively more comfortable with certain approaches over others.

Luckily, everyone can learn to use all the lenses.

A little training—and clear GAME design—goes a long way.

Playbill Analysis

Great leaders ask questions that clearly signal the requested perspective. How did Dee do?

Before we get going, are there any opening remarks?

This inquiry implies no lens, inviting anybody to offer anything. Reid barges in with irrelevant nonsense about room dimensions.

In attempt #2, Dee better articulates the challenge:

We're here to discuss this year's Magical Music Box fundraiser. Let's settle on a clear plan that raises $15,000.

But then she blows it by asking a yes/no question rather than anything productive.

Did you get the agenda?

Effort #3 is better yet.

Why don't we recap last year's event? . . . Let's build on that.

Examining the past is a great tactic. But which lens is requested? A factual analysis (GREEN) or critical evaluation (BLUE/RED)? Ambiguity leaves the floodgates wide open. In many cases, negativity drowns the room, which is exactly the case here. Rip rips:

What's the point of looking back? That was then, this is now.

Magical Music Box needs Great Gaming Goggles, and fast!

Fortunately, this tool can be quickly mastered with minimal training.

Coloring Book

Frustrated with her ineffectual, unproductive team meetings, Dee Cydes knows one thing: It's time to seek help. After her enthusiastic friend Moe Tivayshun raves about his experiences with a tool called *Great Gaming Goggles*, she decides to give it a shot.

When planning her next meeting, Dee maps out two contrasting short GAMEs, limiting each step to a single lens. First, she considers a 60-minute agenda.

CHALLENGE A: Design a fundraising event for a new audience.

CLOCK	ACTIVITY	LENS	PERSPECTIVE
3 min.	**Intro/Welcome** (share Guidelines)		
6 min.	**Which new audiences might we target?**	Purple	Propose
3 min.	**Choose one**	Orange	Own
7 min.	**What motivates this group?**	Green	Gather
10 min.	**What event concepts might get them excited?**	Purple	Propose
4 min.	**Which two should we explore?**	Orange	Own
5 min.	**Develop concepts** (2 subteams, different ideas)	Purple	Propose
3 min.	**Share plans** (90 seconds each)	Green	Gather
3 min.	**What do we like about these proposals?**	Blue	Boost
3 min.	**Any concerns?**	Red	Rip
3 min.	**What are our next steps?**	Purple	Propose

54 min. + buffer

Dee also considers a 30-minute Experience, built around a different angle.

 CHALLENGE B: **How might we improve upon last year's event?**

CLOCK	ACTIVITY	LENS	PERSPECTIVE
2 min.	Intro/Welcome		
5 min.	Summarize last year's event	Green	Gather
3 min.	What went well?	Blue	Boost
3 min.	What didn't?	Red	Rip
9 min.	What might amplify participation?	Purple	Propose
5 min.	Which proposals show promise, and why?	Blue	Boost

27 min. + buffer

These examples offer several important lessons:
- It is common to require the same lens multiple times. (Challenge A incorporates four PURPLEs.)
- A GAME mustn't incorporate all five lenses. (Challenge B omits ORANGE).
- Always leave a buffer. (Challenge A schedules 54/60 minutes. Challenge B assigns 27/30.)

Most people are inherently drawn to one or two lenses. They were simply born a dreamer (PURPLE), analyst (GREEN), or critic (RED). Natural inclinations benefit you and your community, so proudly lean into strengths.

But also commit to improving aptitude with the other perspectives.

To build balanced and effective teams, carefully recruit a combination of orientations.

Innovation requires FIVE glorious **LENSES.** Master them all, but access just one at a time.

CHAPTER **6**

GREEN/GATHER

Puzzlers must become master detectives. Using the GREEN/GATHER lens, hunt for clues, LEARN about crucial aspects (**L**ogistics, **E**motions, **A**ssumptions, **R**esources, **N**arrative), and interpret valuable data.

What can be learned?

GREEN/GATHER

After underwriting a state-of-the-art high-rise, Benny Faktor visits his completed structure for the first time. "It exceeds my wildest dreams!" he raves. "Just one problem. *I'd like it over there—across the street.*"

Oops . . .

How many meaningful projects are forfeited as available resources get overlooked? How many hours are wasted unscrambling previously solved puzzles? How many dollars are squandered . . . opportunities lost . . . communities shattered . . . because core assumptions go untested—until it's too late?

Puzzlers love to dive in and dream. But with partial information or untested suppositions, proposals are notoriously misaligned. They remind me of comedian Victor Borge's line, "My father invented a cure for which there is no disease. (Unfortunately, my mother later caught the cure, and died.)"

Avoid answering before fully comprehending the riddle.

Creative problem solving requires a deep understanding of the world as it is. Innovation champions meticulously gather necessary data, ensuring that building occurs on the right side of the road.

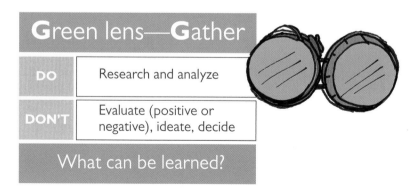

Green lens—**G**ather		
DO	Research and analyze	
DON'T	Evaluate (positive or negative), ideate, decide	
What can be learned?		

Hunt for Clues

Master detectives are meticulous researchers. Careful to note the smallest detail, they painstakingly scrutinize minutiae missed or ignored by others.

Clues are everywhere.

Of course, not every hint proves consequential. Most are dead ends. But on the front end, it is difficult to distinguish duds from deliverables. Data that initially seems insignificant often winds up being noteworthy.

To be safe, overlook nothing. Puzzlers must gather thorough evidence and see where it leads. This may involve learning from teammates, interviewing subjects, researching data, observing up close, and openly welcoming unsolicited insights that fall into your lap.

Tap the Team

Puzzlers in the room represent a logical starting point. In many cases, they were invited precisely because of expertise, institutional history, or logistical know-how. A lot can be learned by looking within, particularly if evaluating the facts.

But for opinions, reactions, or insights, proceed with caution.

It is difficult to simultaneously play scientist and subject.

Double duty introduces inherent conflicts of interest. How can personal biases be objectively assessed?

Talk to Humans

Not every puzzle is human-centric. Some are about science, animals, or art for the sake of art. But most revolve around people. The goal is making life a little better, healthier, more efficient.

Human-centered design engages true experts—the types of individuals you hope to impact. Without their input, major conclusions may be off target, even fatally flawed.

Unfortunately, many communities fail to conduct this imperative research in meaningful ways. Teachers shape curriculum without student input. Businesses take risky gambles before consulting customers, justifying, "We see them everyday!" Members of one demographic naïvely assume their value system resonates equivalently with others.

Whether stemming from lack of time or fear of discovery, this skipped activity notoriously leads to fictional narratives with tarnished conclusions.

Build a listening tour into your GAME.

True, nobody has all the answers. Most of us see the world as it appears, rather than how it could be. Interview subjects are unlikely to envision the elusive feature you've sought for months.

But human beings know a lot. They are uniquely equipped to illuminate *empathy points* (see page 176), articulating what they love and what they don't. These living museums can offer nuanced perspectives on personal habits, passions, fears, hopes, irritations, experiences, aspirations, and impressions.

"The simple truth is that the truth does not exist.
It all depends on a person's point of view."

—Laura Esquivel, Mexican novelist

When studying human behavior,

Check your biases at the door.

If anything, actively seek clues that disprove your intuitive understanding. Enter with a childlike inquisitiveness, a beginner's mindset, as if considering the problem for the first time.

Ask probing questions and dig deep. Be sure to hear what is said—what is intended—carefully reading between the lines. Otherwise, your assumptions, conclusions, and ultimate decisions may be way off the mark.

Seize the Data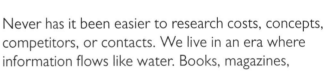

Never has it been easier to research costs, concepts, competitors, or contacts. We live in an era where information flows like water. Books, magazines, journals, and published studies are abundantly available. A simple internet search uncovers countless entries on almost any topic.

The hard part is digging through clutter.

Corroborate all findings. Just because something is written doesn't make it true. Faulty data is particularly rampant online, where unvetted URLs and social media posts are notoriously flooded with gross inaccuracies, biased algorithms, conspiracy theories, and tabloid nonsense (Gasp!).

Look Around

It's one thing to hear about the horrendous conditions of prison, an innovative new lawnmower, or the impeccable customer service of a competitor. But depth of understanding increases exponentially when seeing things with your own eyes.

Take a field trip, letting no detail go unnoticed.

Observe idiosyncrasies, troubling features, charming moments, opportunities for expansion, and anything else that might prove significant.

★ CHALLENGE: Innovate the umbrella.

In a downpour or even a drizzle, life's most cherished possession becomes the umbrella.

Well before dreaming up improvements, inventor Rainey Daze visits parking lots and sporting events while it is showering to observe common inadequacies. Some discoveries:

- Groups struggle to huddle under a single umbrella.
- Shoes are the least protected clothing item.
- When accompanied children hold the handle, the canopy scrapes their adult's head.
- When grasped by grownups, kids are largely unprotected.
- Cheap products often invert or break in strong winds.
- Extended umbrella holding is fatiguing.
- Umbrellas are frequently forgotten when rainfall stops.

One or more of these will ultimately inform his design priorities.

"To acquire knowledge, one must study.
But to acquire wisdom, one must observe."

—Marilyn vos Savant, American playwright

Listen to the Universe

Meaningful clues often present themselves.

Unfortunately, such signs are regularly ignored, discounted, or unrecognized. Puzzlers race toward the future with blinders, unwilling or unable to consider unanticipated gifts.

Many hints come from within.

During casual conversation, a confession slips out: "You know, my dream is . . ." Listen carefully to the words that follow. Stop yourself before a stubborn "*but* . . ." rears its aspiration-sinking head.

An engaged listener asks, "Have you considered X?"

You haven't, and retort the standing proposal with precise explanation. Yet perhaps this isn't the moment for elucidation, but openness to an unexpected prospect.

And then there are obstacles.

At some point, you hit a wall. An agreement falls through. Or the boss drops a definitive "NO!" As panic sets in, you start compromising, determined to prevent complete collapse of the original vision. But what if you flip the equation? How might your closed door unlock better ones?

CLUES hide in the strangest places.

Become an astute, open, hungry observer.

LEARN Before Solving

Many flavors of research are imperative to innovation. Before proposing solutions, LEARN what's necessary for the win.

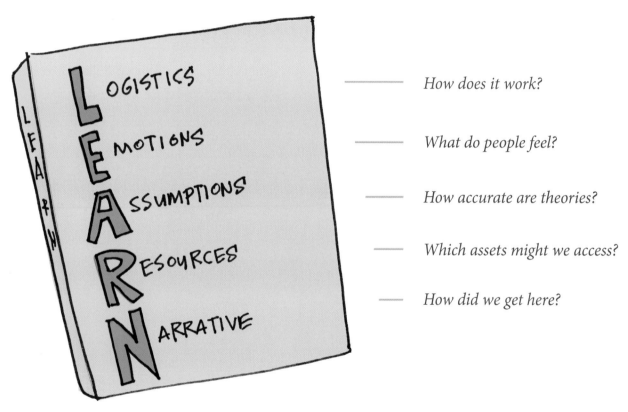

——— *How does it work?*

——— *What do people feel?*

——— *How accurate are theories?*

——— *Which assets might we access?*

——— *How did we get here?*

In the pages that follow, each LEARN consideration is coupled with a specific problem-solving tool.

Many additional devices are also worthy of consideration: SWOT (Strengths, Weaknesses, Opportunities, Threats) analysis, flowcharts and graphs, Venn diagrams. When designing a GAME, consider which techniques are most conducive to mining and organizing needed data.

Logistics

How does it work?

For our purposes, Logistics implies the study of product, service, industry, process, policy, business, or life models.

Before visioning, investigate existing paradigms.

This requires a clear understanding of OUR model (what you currently do, and how) and THEIR model (what the competition does, and how).

sample **LOGISTICS** questions:

- What are the SPECS?
- How is it BUILT?
- How does it RUN?
- How do the PIECES fit together?
- Who are the CUSTOMERS?
- Who are our COMPETITORS, and how do they operate?
- How much does it COST?

Our Model

Nothing occurs in a vacuum. To innovate the future, you must:

Connect the dots between today's reality and tomorrow's promise.

Unfortunately for too many, the magnetic force of current or historic conditions is too strong a bond to break. Any change—no matter how minute— somehow feels threatening, even disrespectful. In fact, the very act of imagining alternatives is uncomfortable.

Yet, as the title of Marshall Goldsmith's book on success articulates, *What Got You Here Won't Get You There*. Or as a core *Puzzler Company* Team Tenet argues (page 286), "Especially today, yesterday rarely describes tomorrow."

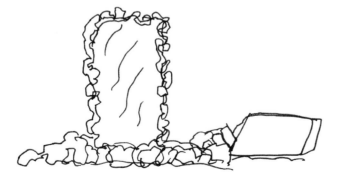

On the flip side, some forward-leaning puzzlers believe it best to blow things up and start from scratch. "The old way is archaic and obsolete!" "A new era deserves new solutions!"

But surely *something* is good about your established approach. Rather than trying to become what you are not, there must be at least a few existing aspects to build upon.

It is crucial to comprehend your status quo before designing a path forward. Detaching emotion, objectively analyze the current state to meaningfully inform later parts of the process, when you may ask:

SPECS

Which aspects should be maintained or tweaked, and what requires revision?

STRENGTHS

How might we amplify current bright spots?

WEAKNESSES

Should liabilities be eliminated, minimized, ignored, repurposed, or reimagined?

Their Model

When making informed, savvy decisions, it is essential to understand the competition, industry norms, and best practices.

- How do others solve this problem?
- Which features or modifications have they introduced?
- What strengths do they bring?
- What weaknesses do they have?
- How are they positioned?

Imitators and innovators often reach opposite conclusions. Copycats believe lessons learned show the optimal way forward. For them, change requires catching up.

But competitive analysis just as often helps pioneers determine what NOT to do.

Understanding the landscape provides a framework to push against. While the masses chase trends like lemmings, these leaders seek a path less travelled.

On the flip side, many puzzlers fritter away untold energy imagining less good alternatives to what already exists. Yet there is no need to reinvent the wheel. (I hoped to avoid clichés, but when in Rome . . .)

Beyond mechanics, use lessons learned to navigate landmines, avoid rookie mistakes, and benefit from successes/failures of others.

Save creative energy for aspects unique to your vision.

Tool: **Metrix Matrix**

Cara's CarWash is struggling. Though demand exists, there's a lot of competition.

 CHALLENGE: Design a compelling competitive advantage.

Before seeking solutions, Team Cara wants to better understand the current landscape. To do this, they design a gridlike *metrix matrix* (next page).

 STEP 1   **Identify entities.**

The team decides to analyze five businesses, shown across the grid's top row:
1. **Us.** Current operating model (1).
2. **Direct competitors.** Rival businesses (2–3).
3. **Intersecting ventures.** Noncompeting, overlapping companies (4–5).

 STEP 2   **Choose parameters to consider.**

Deciding against *price* and *products*, they instead focus on marketing and the user experience, indicated down the left column.

STEP 3   **Research existing approaches.**

Filling in the matrix, entries are concisely stated, often with symbols or pictures.

Later in the process, Team Cara is tasked with determining a powerful *unique selling proposition* (USP) by identifying alternatives to competitors and/or adopting features from noncompeting, intersecting ventures.

Metrix Matrix	Cara's CarWash (our model today)	Vicki's Vehicle Clean	Otto's Auto Wash	Olie's Oil Change	Dora's Dog Salon
Customer Experience	waiting room w/ coffee	hose in hand!	in car	free ride to cafe!	Wi-Fi coffee, cookies, dog treats
Unique Gift Shop Items	standard items only	no gift shop	hats, keychains, gag gifts $$$$!	electronic accessories	locally sourced dog/kid toys
Community Involvement	nope	free washes: *cops & firefighters*	zilch	sponsor local soccer team	supports dog charities
Advertising Beyond Online	billboards	online only	radio, flyers	TV, radio, billboards	zoo/vet/dog park/kennel ads
Loyalty Program	: - (	X	flat rate all-you-can-wash club	6th oil change free	refer a friend, get a gift!

"It's good to have high-quality competition. It helps drive research forward at a faster pace."

—Shuji Nakamura, Japanese engineer and inventor

Emotions

What do people feel?

Here's a radical idea:

If you want to understand how people feel, ask them.

Several layers of introspection may be necessary to uncover truly consequential revelations such as *empathy points*. Ask follow-ups as necessary to clarify context and implications.

EMPATHY POINTS

Elation Points **What DO you love?**	Fantasy Points **What WOULD you love?**	Pain Points **What CAN'T you love?**

Be careful not to confuse solutions with empathy points. "I need a lamp" is a solution. "I can barely see and it's driving me nutty" is a pain point, and one likely to unlock a greater innovation.

sample **EMOTION** questions:

- How do you feel about EXISTING solutions?
- What are you PASSIONATE about, and why?
- What drives you CRAZY, and why?

- How do you deal with those CIRCUMSTANCES?
- What do you wish were DIFFERENT?
- What do you hope NEVER changes?

Tool: *Interview/Focus Group*

Phantastic Pharma is thriving. With profits rising steadily, the employee roster now exceeds 1,500. But not everything is rosy. There is a notable tension across campus, particularly among low-rank workers.

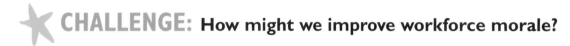

CHALLENGE: **How might we improve workforce morale?**

HR director M. P. Thize and his team commit to upgrading culture. They start by organizing interviews and focus groups, intersecting with a cross-section of departments. Only through probing questions and empathetic listening can they discover what truly resonates and what repels.

The research team agrees upon six priorities for their listening tour:

1. LEARN how people feel before offering solutions.
2. Build bonds early on and smile!
3. Invite comfortable conversation; never interrogate.
4. Arrive with a plan, but be flexible when unexpected clues emerge.
5. Get out of the way! Let subjects do the most talking.
6. Listen, read between the lines, and be sensitive to nonverbal cues.

"Leadership is about empathy. It is about having the ability to relate to and connect with people for the purpose of inspiring and empowering their lives."

—Oprah Winfrey, American talk show host

The 6 Question Classes

Type	Purpose	Description	Example
Rapport	Engagement	Build trust while establishing a friendly, safe space.	*I see a picture of your beautiful family. Have they visited you here?*
Roomy	Interviewee Directed	Broad and flexible, respondents choose the focus.	*What is your favorite/least favorite aspect of this job?*
Restricted	Interviewer Directed	Narrow and specific, limiting the scope of inquiry.	*Can you walk us through your onboarding experience?*
Rate	Evaluation	Quickly gauge priorities with binary (Y/N), multiple choice (a, b, or c), or sliding scale (1–10).	*Do you prefer (a) working alone, (b) with a partner, or (c) on larger teams?*
Retrieval	Follow-Up	Dig deeper into earlier responses.	*You mentioned that department meetings feel like a waste. Have you had any positive experiences?*
Reflection	Exit	Final opportunity to comment.	*Anything else you'd like to share about an ideal work environment?*

During interviews, the team maintains distinct roles. As someone questions, a scribe and a doodler take notes while others observe. Because the same words can be interpreted differently, multiple eyewitnesses are helpful.

Following their listening tour, M. P.'s team analyzes the data. Specifically, they isolate empathy (pain, fantasy, and elation) points mentioned by multiple subjects. These clues may prove pivotal, informing insights, design principles, and ultimately solutions down the road. Some comments that stand out follow.

ELATION points
I DO love . . .

- The beautiful facilities
- Working for a successful company that makes a positive difference
- Several of my colleagues
- Random coffee room encounters

FANTASY points
I WOULD love . . .

- Feeling like I'm part of a family
- Feeling like I am important and valued
- More places to relax during breaks
- Meeting new colleagues
- Doing more purpose-driven work

PAIN points
I CAN'T love . . .

- Feeling invisible, like nobody knows my name
- Feeling underappreciated
- Feeling micromanaged
- Beautiful but impersonal facilities
- Cliques in the workforce
- Not seeing how my work connects to a larger vision
- The gulf between senior leadership and everyone else

To be continued . . . (page 189)

Assumptions

How accurate are theories?

Without assumptions, life would be impossible.

Acts as basic as crossing the street require faith you won't be hit by falling bricks. Yet just because you believe something doesn't make it true. Faulty frameworks and miscalculations cause unnecessary hitches, even entire structures to collapse.

Test key hypotheses early and often.

There are numerous ways to assess critical assumptions: build a prototype, consult with experts, conduct surveys, interview users, verify fact-based items, create an independent but related GAME.

sample ASSUMPTIONS:

- PRODUCTION will be completed within eight months.
- We will be granted A PATENT / APPROVAL.
- Our "VIRAL" campaign will actually catch fire.
- PARTNERS will care as much as we do.
- START-UP COSTS will be under $120,000.
- Clients will PAY $37.
- People will CARE.

"Assumptions are dangerous things."

—Agatha Christie, British mystery novelist

Tool: *Survey*

For years, vocalist Melody Crafter has composed personalized tunes for family and friends. Now she hopes to turn it into a business.

 CHALLENGE: Launch a custom lullabye venture.

Melody suspects well-to-do clients will eagerly invest in this unique luxury item. But that's based on little more than a hunch. To find out, she creates a survey.

Many puzzlers misunderstand this tool. They mistakenly believe the goal is generating positive feedback. Though such validation feels great, the primary objective should be to test assumptions and learn.

Honest reaction beats hollow affirmation.

Melody begins by identifying assumptions critical to her business model:

A. People will LOVE the idea of custom lullabies.

B. My primary audience is wealthy, older women.

C. Customers will pay a $3,000 commissioning fee.

D. Lullabies will be most popular as a GIFT for young children.

E. Consumers will want to customize something beyond the recipient's name appearing in lyrics (but what?).

When designing her survey, Melody is struck by the psychological significance of even minor wording variation. The question itself can bias respondents, thus tainting accuracy. For example, here are five ways to ask about pricing. Consider how different each feels.

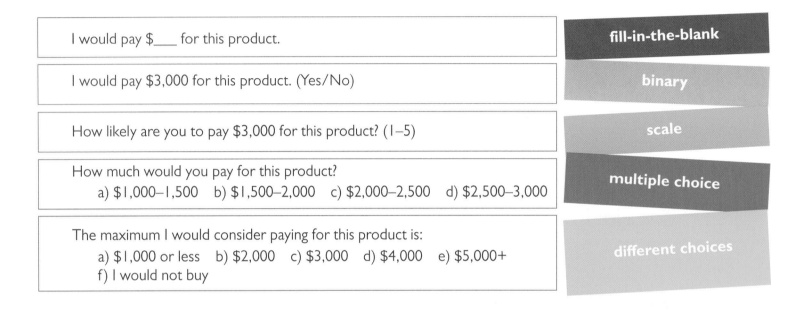

I would pay $____ for this product.	**fill-in-the-blank**
I would pay $3,000 for this product. (Yes/No)	**binary**
How likely are you to pay $3,000 for this product? (1–5)	**scale**
How much would you pay for this product? a) $1,000–1,500 b) $1,500–2,000 c) $2,000–2,500 d) $2,500–3,000	**multiple choice**
The maximum I would consider paying for this product is: a) $1,000 or less b) $2,000 c) $3,000 d) $4,000 e) $5,000+ f) I would not buy	**different choices**

Melody's ultimate survey, shown on the next page, is distributed through social media, retirement homes, business communities, and a baby expo.

Note how every question tests an assumption.*

An analysis of 230 responses proves invaluable. Several suspicions are confirmed, with others challenged. The most notable revelation involves price. While most interested folks would pay only the low end, 18 surveys indicate a willingness to disburse $4,000 or more! More than just a blip, this convinces Melody to raise her rate—and message of exclusivity.

Assumption indications on the next page are for explanation only. They do not appear on actual survey.

Melody's CUSTOM Lullabies
Survey

1. Your gender:

☐ Male
☐ Female

2. Your age: _____

3. Annual household income:

a. Less than $50,000
b. $50,000–75,000
c. $75,000–100,000
d. $100,000–150,000
e. Over $150,000

About us:

Do you seek a one-of-a-kind, personalized, luxury gift? Award-winning singer-songwriter Melody Crafter will compose a beautiful 3 minute lullaby dedicated to your special somebody. Play the recording every day, and give a gift that lasts a lifetime!

4. On a scale of 1–5, how interested are you in this exclusive gift item? (1 = not at all interested, 5 = extremely interested)

1   2   3   4   5

TESTED ASSUMPTIONS:

1 = B
2 = B
3 = B
4 = A
5 = D
6 = E
7 = C
8 = E

See page 181

---

5. Who would be the most likely recipient? (check all that apply)

☐ My child/grandchild
☐ Child of a friend
☐ Significant other
☐ Parent
☐ Myself
☐ Someone else: _____

6. All lullabies prominently feature the recipient's name. What else would you hope to customize? (choose one)

a. Personal details in the lyrics
b. Meaningful quotes/messages in the lyrics
c. Musical style
d. Music video featuring a photomontage
e. The name is enough, just make it beautiful!

7. The maximum I would consider paying for this personalized, exclusive product is:

a. $1,000 or less   b. $2,000   c. $3,000
d. $4,000   e. $5,000+   f. I wouldn't buy.

8. How might this gift be even more meaningful?

_____

Resources

Which assets might we access?

A great idea is rarely enough. Bringing it to fruition requires assistance: people, partners, money, publicity, infrastructure. Though identifying such opportunities may be a challenge, there is good news.

More resources than initially apparent are often accessible.

Tool: *Mind Map*

While visiting an African village, Phil N. Thropist makes a troubling discovery. Many adults are severely sight impaired, yet nothing is being done to improve their situation.

 CHALLENGE: Provide eyeglasses to Nuzoma villagers (as soon as possible!).

Back home in Waterton, Phil meets some friends to address this challenge. None are directly affiliated with the cause, and at first they feel stymied. But following some research, puzzlers are excited to discover numerous potential resources. Specifically, the team considers four asset categories:

1. Used eyeglass *collectors* (Waterton)
2. Possible *couriers* already traveling to Nuzoma region
3. Potential *distribution* centers within the village
4. Vision *diagnosis* tools (despite limited Wi-Fi and electricity)

sample **RESOURCE** questions:

- WHO do we know?
- Which INFLUENCERS (organizations, experts, volunteers, etc.) can be engaged?
- What FUNDING sources are within reach?
- Are there PLATFORMS we might leverage?
- Might we borrow SPACES (materials, supplies, equipment, etc.)?

Phil's team reveals findings with a mind map, using the following instructions. Integrating words and pictures, this tool illustrates interrelated concepts on a single page.

- Central image showcases main idea.
- Multiple fields highlight asset categories.
- Entries are added within each field.
- Connections are made with branches of various thicknesses.
- Make it personal!

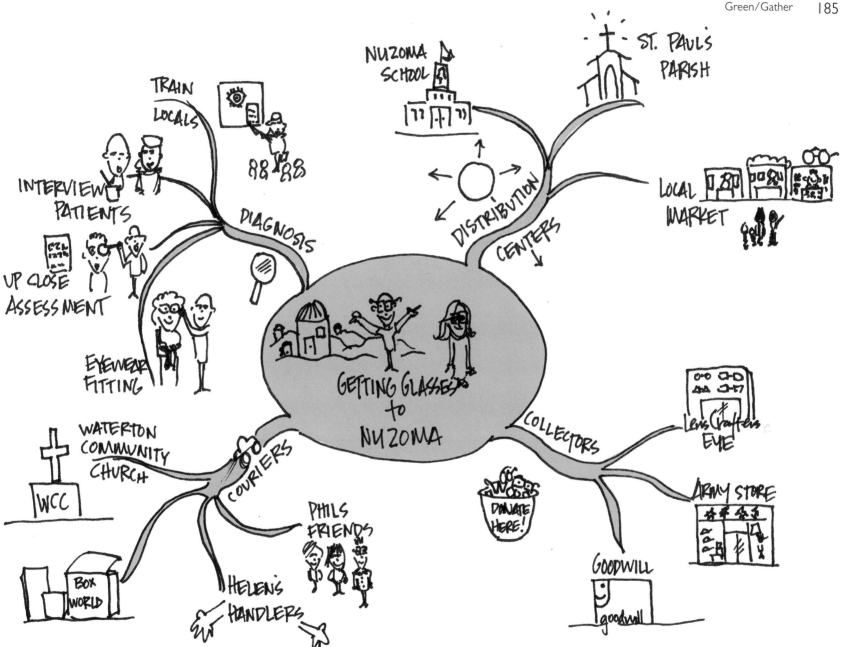

Narrative

How did we get here?

Nothing exists in a vacuum. Examine past and current realities for context, elucidating a starting point, historic winners/losers, and potential hazards.

Just because something previously succeeded or failed doesn't mean history will repeat itself. However, the why, how, and what of precedent offer essential data. With the benefit of hindsight, it is possible to analyze cause-and-effect relationships.

When inconvenient facts bump against your preformed narrative, resist the urge to suppress. In fact, *remove your views completely*. Follow facts by conducting objective, nuanced reconnaissance.

Every story has multiple sides.

sample **NARRATIVE** questions:

- For better or worse, what are the DYNAMICS today?
- WHY do we do things this way?
- HOW did we get here?
- How has this problem been addressed PREVIOUSLY?
- What OBSTACLES have prevented success?
- Which CIRCUMSTANCES are different now?

Tool: *Storyboard*

For decades, tension has grown between police and the African American community of Frictionville. Both groups view one another with suspicion and fear.

A new commissioner, Harmony Helper, is determined to turn things around.

 CHALLENGE: Build trust between police and the community.

To start, she insists on understanding the jagged history connecting these groups. An empathetic, neutral team interviews stakeholders representing *both* perspectives. Major incidents informing public opinion are documented through a storyboard. Visuals illustrate this complex narrative better than words alone.

CITIZEN perspective

| 1967, police arrest protesters | 1985, police rough up a pair of young Black men | 2021, police harass Black teen without cause |

POLICE perspective

| 1967, rioters loot neighborhood | 1984, rocks thrown at patrol car | 2019, gun violence rises in Black neighborhood |

Interpret the Data

Detectives do more than collect data. They make sense of it all.

Sort and Connect

In crime dramas, there's often a scene featuring investigators huddled in a room. Clues—photographs, receipts, newspaper clippings, maps—are attached asymmetrically to a designated bulletin board or wall. Yarn zigzags from item to item, suggesting possible connections.

Similarly, many innovation GAME activities generate mountains of evidence or proposals. Sort them with a GREEN lens. *No new material, critique, or decisions allowed at this time.*

SHOWCASE	**CLUSTER**	**ELIMINATE**	**TITLE**
Find a wall, table, or other large space.	Group closely related ideas.	Remove redundant/ unnecessary entries.	Add umbrella names to each cluster group.

  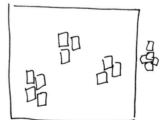 

"The goal is to turn data into information and information into insight."

—Carly Fiorina, American businesswoman and politician

Identify Insights

Innovation often stems from insights discovered during GREEN lens research.

Insights are not hard facts, data, or statistics (though this information can lead to one). Rather, they encapsulate shrewd revelations and observations. Whether clarifying underlying conditions, why previous attempts failed, or what subjects hope to feel:

Insights represent 'a-ha!' breakthroughs.

The best examples are captured in simple, easy to understand statements. They trigger you and your team to approach the puzzle in fresh ways.

Interviews around Phantastic Pharma's workforce morale bugaboo (page 179) generated a number of actionable lessons. Several came in the form of direct insights—surprising, standalone statements wrapped in a bow.

I DO love . . . Random coffee room encounters.

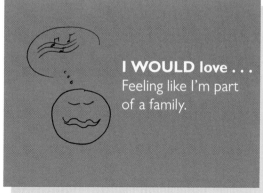

I WOULD love . . . Feeling like I'm part of a family.

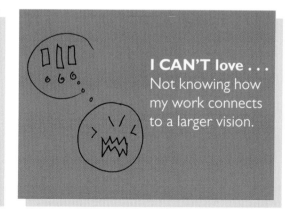

I CAN'T love . . . Not knowing how my work connects to a larger vision.

Connecting two or more previously disassociated dots, *multipoint insights* lead to deeper enlightenment. Try various combinations to discover truly intriguing epiphanies.

$$A+B=I$$

(Empathy Point A + Empathy Point B = Insight)

PAIN POINT A: ELATION POINT B: **INSIGHT #1**	Employees can't love feeling INVISIBLE. They do love working in BEAUTIFUL FACILITIES. **Attractive public spaces should celebrate staff contributions.**
ELATION POINT A: PAIN POINT B: **INSIGHT #2:**	Employees do love working for a SUCCESSFUL COMPANY that makes a positive difference. They can't love feeling like contributions LACK PURPOSE. **Employees should meet satisfied customers** (seeing the end result of a process in which they are essential).
FANTASY POINT A: FANTASY POINT B: ELATION POINT C: **INSIGHT #3:**	Employees would love feeling like they're PART OF A FAMILY. They would love MEETING NEW COLLEAGUES. They do love COFFEE ROOM ENCOUNTERS. **Coffee rooms should create community, mixing staff from across the organization.**

Reframe the GAME

Come time for solutioning, critical insights should be weighed heavily. In fact, they are so important, you may want to reframe the challenge mid-GAME.

The original Phantastic Pharma premise was quite broad.

 ## CHALLENGE:

How might we improve workforce morale?

Considering insights from the last page, a variety of new challenge statements might be considered.

REFRAME 1:	Design a vibrant public space that celebrates staff.
REFRAME 2:	Design an initiative that introduces employees to happy customers.
REFRAME 3:	Design coffee cohorts that mix staff from across the organization.
REFRAME 1 + 2:	Design a dynamic area where employees and satisfied customers meet.
REFRAME 1 + 3:	Design a vibrant public space where coffee cohorts can meet.
REFRAME 2 + 3:	Design coffee cohorts for employees and satisfied customers.

■ Approach innovation with the resolve of a detective.

GATHER data, test assumptions, and learn from humans.

7

PURPLE/PROPOSE

Innovation requires imagination. Using the PURPLE/PROPOSE lens, remember seven brainstorming rules, apply these 10 creative catalysts, and prototype your vision.

What can be imagined?

PURPLE/PROPOSE

To the outsider, breakthrough proposals can feel like magic. *Poof.* Inexplicably, a spellbinding revelation appears. Challenging the status quo, some jaw-dropping vision achieves profound success in ways previously inconceivable. The wizard behind the curtain is heralded for brilliance and supernatural ability.

This is how so many of us view the likes of Thomas Edison, Martha Graham, Maya Angelou, Steve Jobs, Marie Curie, Nelson Mandella, Walt Disney. It's what we feel when innovators' groundbreaking epiphanies disrupt the market or invade our home. These creative geniuses were born with great minds.

"But me? My organization? We simply don't possess the gift."

True, some human beings are inherently more inventive than others. That said,

Creativity—like magic— is not actually magic.

Innovation champions have more than miracle Eureka moments. They possess a toolbox of tricks for stimulating the imagination. Luckily, many techniques can be learned.

Purple lens—**P**ropose	
DO	Envision creative ideas or content
DON'T	Research, evaluate (positive or negative), decide
What can be imagined?	

Brainstorming Rules

Brilliant solutions rarely appear as instantaneous light-bulbs. Creative envisioning starts with a brainstorm.

Asked to list brainstorming protocols, good-hearted puzzlers often declare, "There are no rules! Tear off the shackles!" Though many groups seem to follow this mantra, anarchy is not recommended. Be sure your team understands how this game is played.

RULE 2: Critique Not

Keep brainstorming judgment-free. Negative (RED lens) feedback is strictly prohibited, since it robs time and carries a psychological price tag. A lack of safe space causes puzzlers to retreat. And who knows? Even proposals that initially feel shaky may grow on you.

RULE 1: More, Not Better

Brainstorming requires MANY ideas, not securing a Nobel Prize. The initial 5–10 proposals are typically obvious—share them quickly and advance to more intriguing terrain. Fifty-nine flawed options beats a single, perfect nugget. (Incidentally, with 59 entries, odds are high that several have potential!) To force abundance, set count minimums (e.g., you must generate at least 25 ideas).

Quantity over quality!

this thing sucks

RULE 3: Zip It

To maximize quantity, be brief. Reveal and get out of the way. This is not the time for attention to detail. Many ideas can be initially captured in 1–4 words. No complete sentences or flowery adjectives required.

Rule 4: **It's All Good . . .**

There are no bad ideas when brainstorming. (Actually, there are two: having none and failing to communicate!) Subpar inklings aren't useless. Even catastrophic notions may be transformed into gems.

Rule 5: **Get Wild & Crazy**

When someone states, "OK, this idea is insane," listen up! Innovation may be on the lurch. Celebrate the bold and uncommon. Even over-the-top, unrealistic suggestions may be tamed to feasibility.

For extraordinary results, don't shut out "the impossible."

Rule 6: **Build Under, Over, & Around**

Proposals are building blocks. Create new shapes by stacking ideas on top, burrowing underneath, or expanding to the side. Word association, "yes, and" statements, and one-upsmanship are fruitful.

Rule 7: **Keep It Fun**

Enjoy the process! It is difficult to explore freely when stress pounds at the door. A quick "great idea!" or pat on the back build self-confidence. Laughter elevates rapport. Imagination flourishes within positive, nurturing environments.

"It's an attitude of not just thinking outside the box, but not even seeing the box."

—Safra A. Catz, Israeli American CEO of Oracle Corporation

10 Creative Catalysts

Innovators don't merely arrive at better solutions. They ask better questions, and with good cause.

How you ask the question impacts the answer.

Most people ask *boring* questions. As a result, they arrive at dull, normal, predictable solutions.

The least inspired query of all: "What should we do?" This certainly isn't terrible. In fact, it's the very reason you're here. But it lacks energy and is unlikely to inspire artistic invention.

Intriguing questions prompt intriguing answers.

If seeking the ambitious, spectacular, distinguished, or just plain weird, design your query accordingly.

So rather than posing . . .

What should we have for lunch today?

Try something with more charm, more ambition, more *je ne sais quois* . . .

What should we have for lunch today that will make us smile in 30 years?

This chapter introduces 10 *creative catalysts*—techniques that activate the imagination.

1. "Q" Variations
2. Change the Frame
3. Obstacle Storming
4. Feature Tweaking
5. Concept Collision
6. Goal Amplification
7. Value Amplification
8. Narrowing
9. Disaster Storming
10. No Shows

"A beautiful question shifts the way we think about something and often sets in motion a process that can result in change."

—Warren Berger, American author of *A More Beautiful Question*

1: "Q" Variations

Remarkable though it may be,

One question goes only so far.

It requires multiple attempts to shake down ideas buried deep within the mind. Introducing a succession of prompts, pose the scenario backward, upside down, inside out, and from the side.

⭐ **CHALLENGE: Design highly unique vacation packages.**

Faye Kation's tour company plans to introduce a new line of unforgettable itineraries. Planning is half the fun. The team has 3 minutes to brainstorm each of the following.

What vacation experiences:

1. Are like a dream?
2. Push people out of their comfort zones?
3. Relate to ancient history?
4. Have never crossed your mind?
5. Help guests meet intriguing, racially diverse people?
6. Teach uncommon skills?
7. Are underground or high in the air?
8. Involve sand/chocolate/animals/high rises?
9. Integrate activities with five letters?

The process results in almost 125 Post-its, including uncommon but appealing prospects. From there, puzzlers debate the merits of promising proposals.

2: Change the Frame

Kick-start your imagination with wild, extreme, even weird premises.

⭐ **CHALLENGE: Make our product go viral.**

Buzz Worthy wants his new widget to catch fire. Rather than simply mining for solutions, he poses nine absurd questions.

What if we:

1. Had one million dollars?
2. Used the widget to raise a million dollars?
3. Collaborated with a prison?
4. Partnered with a mega-movie star?
5. Had an underwater store?
6. Marketed primarily to squirrels?
7. Launched on the moon?
8. Lived in the mid-1700s?
9. Were transported 50 years into the future?

Buzz brings things back to Earth during a later phase. "Since we don't actually have $1,000,000/live in the future, how might proposals be adjusted for reality?"

"A wise man can learn more from a foolish question than a fool can learn from a wise answer."

—Bruce Lee, Hong Kongese martial artist, actor, director

3: Obstacle Storming

Puzzlers often volunteer solutions before fully comprehending—or even considering—roadblocks. As a result, mismatched conclusions are flawed or superficial, failing to appreciably improve the situation.

The following two-step technique uses obstacles as a departure to innovation.

 CHALLENGE: **Triple our audience size.**

Ballet Boop Dance performs in a 450-seat venue. Unfortunately, audience attendance averages just 150.

To increase income and impact, what might they do?

STEP 1   **Identify obstacles.**

Which hurdles prevent goals from being reached? In this case, there are two populations to consider:

1. Ballet lovers who don't currently attend.
2. People NOT interested in ballet who don't currently attend (a much larger pool).

STEP 2   **Imagine solutions.**

To force creativity, the Ballet Boop team must reach a proposal quota: four solutions to counteract each obstacle.

How might you expand each list to eight?

SMALL BALLET AUDIENCE

OBSTACLES	SOLUTIONS	OBSTACLES	SOLUTIONS
SCHEDULING CONFLICTS/ PEOPLE TOO BUSY	1. Choose better night 2. Built-in audiences (schools, conferences) 3. "Time-management" themed show 4. Be more compelling than conflicts	COMMUTE + PARKING = ANNOYING	1. Livestream events (watch from home) 2. Audio program notes (listen during commute) 3. Bus from garage to venue w/preshow 4. Ticket includes Uber!
TICKETS TOO EXPENSIVE	1. Lower price 2. "Buy one, give one," to low-income folks 3. Groupon offers 4. Give away 100 tickets to local orgs (after all, seats are empty)	CHILD CARE EXPENSIVE/ DIFFICULT	1. Childcare at event (included in price) 2. Simultaneous dance class for kids 3. Family-oriented performances 4. Local kids in show
DON'T WANT TO ATTEND ALONE	1. Buy one, get one free tickets 2. Singles mixer 3. Service for introducing single-ticket holders 4. Market to large groups	NO CONNECTION TO ART/ARTISTS	1. Theme about something they DO care about (e.g., football) 2. Dancers mingle w/ audience 3. Dancers build ties w/ community orgs 4. Role for local "celebs"

4: Feature Tweaking

The first time something is tried, it appears revolutionary. The third repetition is fresh. The tenth example is trendy. The hundredth is commonplace. The thousandth is archaic.

Innovation is contextual.

It's amazing how little variation exists in just about any sector. Standing apart may require little more than altering a feature or two.

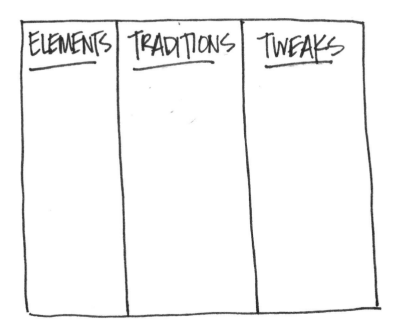

⭐ **CHALLENGE: Design a fun, unique restaurant concept.**

Entrepreneur Abby Tizer plans to open an eatery in a neighborhood packed with options. More important than cuisine type is introducing a highly differentiated, buzzworthy approach.

Before brainstorming, she asks her team to divide a large paper into thirds.

STEP 1   **Classify elements.**

What activity categories are necessary?

In the leftmost column, list general activity categories. No solutions allowed at this point, just elements. The group identifies:

1. FOOD PREPARATION
2. SEATING ARRANGEMENTS
3. ORDERING

STEP 2   Identify traditions.

How are elements normally approached?

In the middle, indicate typical solutions. It turns out that even in a world abundant with options, most manage things similarly. For FOOD PREPARATION they list:

    a. Cooked by anonymous chef
    b. Prepared in closed kitchen

STEP 3   Imagine tweaks.

What might be done differently?

On the right, explore alternatives. Abby stresses the value of even wild ideas. If proposals seem ridiculous, impossible, or just plain wrong, worry not. *Never judge.*

She reminds puzzlers to keep entries concise and requires three tweaks per tradition. (Of course, *idea equity* isn't necessary. A process might allow 13 concepts for one category while another is left blank.)

Note the importance of middle column wording. For example, "Cooked by anonymous chef" offers three points of inspiration:

"Cooked"	What if food weren't cooked, but raw?
"Anonymous"	What if you met the chef?
"Chef"	Who else might prepare the meal?

> *"Every time someone gives you a formula for what you should be and what you should do, know they're giving you a pair of handcuffs."*
>
> —Junot Diaz, Dominican American writer

Feature Tweaking: *Restaurant Innovations*

ELEMENTS	TRADITIONS	TWEAKS
FOOD PREPARATION	• Cooked by anonymous chef • Prepared in closed kitchen	• Raw foods only • Meet the chef • Cooked by customer, waitstaff, local celeb, robots, etc. • Prepped in open kitchen • Prepped @ table • Prepped in fire pit
SEATING ARRANGEMENTS	• Sit at tables/booths • One party per table	• Sit on floor • Sit on beds, boats, hammocks, in pool, etc. • Stand and eat • Community tables • Private eating "desks" • Groups broken up, communicate via video chat
ORDERING	• View paper menu • Order via wait staff	• No menu; waiter chooses • Menus on crayon box, plate bottom, floor, waiter tattoo(!) • Hologram/scratch 'n' sniff menu • Fixed menu, no ordering • Ordering app • Call chef, dial phone

5: Concept Collision

Most of us seek guidance from same-sector relatives. Clowns apprentice clowns; lawyers look to law firms; car dealers attend automotive conventions.

But breakthrough solutions most often occur when one world bumps into another. Inspiration can be found in the strangest of places.

Seek the "wrong" role models.

 CHALLENGE: How might we invigorate our fashion business?

Taylor Fashun wants to try something bold with his struggling clothing store. Rather than emulating direct competitors, he looks outside the bubble for clues.

BEFORE PLAY — Identify successful, noncompeting entities.

When designing his GAME, Taylor writes the name of 30 successful entities on individual *concept cards*.

Disney World
IKEA
Broadway
Star Wars
YouTube
Olympics
Mystery Theatre
Cookbooks
iPhones
Netflix
Video Games
Christmas
Starbucks
Southwest Air
Zoos
Amazon

Kindergarten
Ben & Jerry's
National Parks
Facebook
Sushi
Coca-Cola
Bowling Alleys
Cirque du Soleil
Farmers Markets
Block Parties
Comic Books
Reality TV
Uber
Prius/Hybrids
Shoes
Food Trucks

STEP 1

Consider their success strategies.

During play, multiple teams draw concept cards from a bag and then articulate intriguing principles that help each thrive.

STEP 2

Imagine ways to adopt to your model.

Puzzlers then consider how discoveries might transfer to the fashion business.

A few proposals follow.

MYSTERY THEATRE

Exciting who-done-it entertainment.

FASHION STORE

Mystery play in our store; characters wear inventory as costumes.

KINDERGARTEN

Student artwork showcased on walls (developing community pride).

FASHION STORE

Customer photos showcased on walls (developing community pride).

OLYMPICS

Televised, skill-based competitions.

FASHION STORE

Locally televised event where customers model three outfits and compete before judges.

FOOD TRUCKS

Mobile restaurants for lunch.

FASHION STORE

Mobile fashion shows.

UBER

Through Uber Eats, drivers are hired to conveniently deliver takeout orders from local chain restaurants.

FASHION STORE

Through Uber Fashion, drivers are hired to conveniently deliver clothing items to local customers.

6: Goal Amplification

"What are your dreams?"

I asked this question to a group of college freshmen. Some cited grandiose ambitions. Others were more modest. But all had eyes on some sort of prize.

A follow-up: "In five years, will your dreams be bigger or smaller?" The response was unanimous: "SMALLER!"

"And what if I had asked the question 10 years ago?" Another unison: "BIGGER!"

Back then, they wanted to visit the moon, become president, cure cancer. Heck, as a second grader, my daughter hoped to marry Darth Vader!

Why is it that as we age, ambitions shrink?

Most often, instincts downsize as reality sets in. Urgency skyrockets. Sure, it would be amazing to change the world! But for now I just need to get by . . .

Rather than shrugging shoulders and diminishing expectations, another approach holds promise.

If a puzzle feels too difficult, try making it BIGGER.

"How high does a sycamore grow? If you cut it down, then you'll never know."

—Pocahontas, Native American Powhatan

Any quantifiable goal can be multiplied: target income, number of customers, neighborhoods served, sales, social media followers, and so on.

Here's a process:

Articulate current number.

Project a (significantly) higher number.

Propose solutions to reach that goal.

 CHALLENGE: Fundraise $3,000.

For over a decade, Hitting High Volleyball Team (HHVT) raised up to $2,500 annually through a bake sale and car wash.

This season, they hope to generate more. Their stretch goal of $3,000 feels ambitious, even daunting.

Yet from another perspective, $500 represents a small increase. While success may be possible, it is unlikely that bold, alternative approaches will be considered—let alone adopted—as they plan the strategy.

With modest/incremental goals, most puzzlers pursue what they've always done, only slightly better.

What if HHVT changes the construct, doubling their target to $5,000? Making such a dramatic leap requires a strategic overhaul.

And even falling short by bringing in just $4,600 far exceeds the initial $3,000 aspiration!

When amplifying goals, success may be possible even in failure.

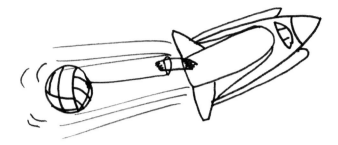

Amplified aspirations force radical reimagination.

How might amplification shape strategy? Note the correlation between heightened ambition and creativity. Here are four of a hundred solutions.

Joust-a-thon	During halftime of a school basketball game, the volleyball team emerges. Previously secured donors offer $1 per consecutive volley over 100 seconds. The results: 60 pledges × $1/hit × 75 volleys = **$4,500** (in 100 seconds!)
Spikes, Spikes, & Spikes	This ticketed, black-tie event is a fashion show featuring local celebrities serving spiked drinks (donated), sporting spiked haircuts, wearing spiked heels. 150 guests × $50/person = **$7,500**
Verbal Volley	HHVT is the opening act for a high-profile rap concert in a local 12,000-seat arena. The team competes against performing artists. $6,000 appearance fee + $5,000 share of concessions = **$11,000**
Lunar Volleyball	HHVT sends their team ball—signed by astronauts— on a space shuttle mission, scheduled in tandem with an eclipse. Auctioned after returning to Earth. **$50,000** auction price plus international media attention

7: Value Amplification

Amplification is also powerful when applied to beliefs and objectives.

How might you multiply existing values?

★ **CHALLENGE: Make student recitals awesome!**

Phil Harmonik runs a music teaching academy that is looking to shake up their events.

STEP 1   **Identify current features/values.**

Phil's team identifies four aspects that have traditionally played a role:

1. STUDENT INVOLVEMENT in a live performance.
2. Performers must be FLEXIBLE IN THE MOMENT.
3. COMMUNITY BUILDING occurs.
4. FAMILY ENGAGEMENT is encouraged.

STEP 2   **Describe traditional role(s).**

They continue by substantiating how each value is currently/traditionally emphasized.

STEP 3   **Imagine amplified role(s).**

Magnifying the impact of each goal generates a host of fresh ideas.

Student Involvement

Traditional	Amplified
Students: • Play instrument/ sing for audience	Students: • Write program notes • Provide verbal intros to music they perform • Make video intros • Design the "set," program order, reception, etc.

Flexibility in the Moment

Traditional	Amplified
• Operate in a new venue • Adopt to new performance conditions • Adjust if memory slip/ mistake occurs	• Program order drawn from hat • Improvisations • Audience members suggest parameters (loud, slow, high, etc.) • Sight-reading recitals (see music the first time in concert)

Community Building

Traditional	Amplified
Audience: • Sit together to enjoy event • Mingle before and after, possibly at reception	Audience: • Dress in costume, related to theme • Participate (sing-along, clapping in time, call & response) • Share strategies for maintaining musical home • Adults vs. kids "cheering" competition (hint: kids will win)

Family Engagement

Traditional	Amplified
Family members: • Attend recital • Listen adoringly • Unwrap cough drops • Applaud	Family members: • Perform collaboratively • Given parent-of-the-year award • Introduce performers (hobbies, anecdotes) • Prepare reception dishes • Contribute to studio cookbook (w/bios, photos, & favorite tunes!)

8: Narrowing

Ambitious puzzlers want it all. The audience is *everyone!* The focus is *everywhere!* The product does *everything!*

Here's the problem:

Being all things to all people equals nothing to nobody.

Unless you're Amazon, it's an unwieldy, counterproductive, likely doomed posture. There is a better way.

Get SMALL to grow BIG.

Targeting a narrow *niche* can augment other aspirations. In fact, amplifying and narrowing often work hand in hand.

- A magazine amplifies readership by narrowing focus (making it extremely pertinent to one group).
- A museum amplifies demand by narrowing what it showcases.
- A public speaker amplifies gigs after becoming "famous" for a specific message.
- A store amplifies customer engagement after limiting items sold, making their value incredibly relevant to one target segment.

 CHALLENGE: What if we sell puzzles?

Suppose *The Puzzler Company*, my consulting team, explores a new revenue model.

Our initial plan includes puzzles of all sorts: famous people, natural beauty, historic paintings, aardvarks. But doing so adds our brand to a long list of historic competitors who already dominate market share.

Instead we narrow. How might we own a niche? Simply asking the question helps us focus.

Perhaps we decide that Puzzler Puzzles showcase only our own innovation methodology. This specialty product isn't for everyone. But for a certain kind of human—including those who would never otherwise buy interlocking cardboard pieces—such uniqueness holds intrigue.

9: Disaster Storming

I've argued, "there are no bad ideas" when brainstorming. This is no time for condemnatory judgment.

But what about terrible ideas?

True calamities carry energy. They trigger wincing, flinching, radioactive stomach pits. Though mediocre notions (or even good ones) may be greeted with apathy, there is no neutral when flirting with catastrophe.

CHALLENGE: How might we improve the onboarding experience?

Kori Peration is the new branch manager. During her "listening tour," several new hires confess to feeling isolated and lost. So she organizes a short innovation GAME.

STEP 1   **Imagine terrible ideas**

Kori divides 35 employees into several groups. Positioned at flip charts, they are asked to brainstorm dreadful, appalling, even borderline-offensive notions.

Some proposals include:
- Parking lot lines removed
- Meetings while standing on one foot
- "Formal Fridays"
- "Take a Stranger to Work Day"
- Lock bathroom doors
- No desks or chairs
- Garlic lunches
- Random breath screening (following garlic)
- Copy machine accepts only sandpaper
- New office location every day
- Executive leader boxing match
- Meetings staged as Broadway Musical

214

STEP 2   **Select one.**

Rotate stations and inherit lists from predecessors. Then select the most *cringeworthy* concept.

STEP 3   **Transform into a terrific idea.**

Using the step 2 selection as inspiration, teams imagine a truly remarkable onboarding initiative, defining the details.

STEP 4   **Judges choose their favorite.**

Assistant managers B. Sniss, M. Pire, and N. Dustry judge the competition. The winning pitch follows.

TERRIBLE IDEA: New office location every day.

TERRIFIC IDEA: It is crucial to get new employees quickly integrated into office culture. This requires meaningful exchanges beyond the customary meet-and-greet.

Instead of cubicles, our system assigns a "pod" to each new hire. While this workspace offers all the amenities of a traditional office, it comes with a twist.

Pods are on movable platforms.

After hours, they are rearranged randomly. Each morning, recent employees must find their new location. Personal items stand out and serve as conversation starters.

Seasoned workers help colleagues find their spot (figuratively and physically). New positioning prompts networking with fresh faces across department and rank while building trust, communication, and camaraderie.

10: No Shows

Following a brainstorm or innovation GAME, it is instructive to review the wealth of proposals. Representing the collective wisdom, entries mean at least one puzzler thought along those lines.

Equally fascinating: angles that are absent. Such exclusions frequently represent vast gulfs of opportunity. Thanks to untested assumptions, groupthink, or a failure to ask the right questions, omissions guarantee even promising directions receive NO hearing.

To illuminate the invisible, take a second look.

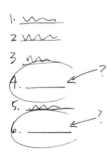

What have we missed?

A more dramatic approach removes current suggestions from consideration (at least temporarily). "That's an impressive list! Now suppose those solutions are off limits. Then what?"

CHALLENGE: Transform our high school into a model of excellence.

Following decades of declining performance, a failing school hires consultant Dr. Fixit to turn things around.

Meeting with the entire staff, Fixit asks, "What considerations determine school success?" Answers include graduation rates, grades, standardized test scores, attendence, college readiness/acceptance, student conduct, teacher retention. "Anything else?" Silence.

"Clearly, these issues are of utmost importance. They must remain top of mind. Having identified them, we can now build strategies."

Following a deep breath, he continues: "Now let's try again. What potentially important metrics didn't make our initial brainstorm? What else contributes to school success?"

Following an awkward pause, suggestions start to flow. "Parent engagement." "Expanded internet." "Summer learning." "Student curricular choices." "Community partnerships." "Interdisciplinary collaboration."

When it comes to innovation, No Shows frequently provide the most illuminating guidance.

Prototyping Innovation

Innovation entails more than BIG ideas and isolated solutions. It requires working through details, determining which features matter most and how they fit together. For that reason, many GAMEs involve *prototyping*.

The time frame and nature of each challenge affect what is possible. Prototyping often involves the types of Materials found on page 98.

Prototype examples:

- 3D models
- Sketches
- Image rendering
- Posters
- Brochures

- Timelines
- Spec sheets
- Storyboards
- Videos
- Sample experiences

Building a tangible creation forces puzzlers to get specific. It demands attention to structural properties easily overlooked when ideas reside only in the mind. Prototyping strengthens the vision while grounding puzzlers in reality.

Mock-ups should be shared and critiqued.

The usefulness of verbal description alone is limited. It is easier for reviewers to accurately perceive that which can be seen and touched. User feedback becomes exponentially more insightful when studying/testing physical artifacts.

"I made 5,127 prototypes of my vacuum before I got it right."

—James Dyson, British inventor

Minimum Viable Product

Perfectionism runs rampant. We resist sharing projects before they're refined, edited, and complete with bells and whistles. Weeks, months, or years evaporate before unveiling our impeccable masterpiece.

That's unfortunate. How do you know if ideas are any good without collecting feedback?

Waiting too long to test an idea increases the likelihood of structural flaws, untested assumptions, and wasted energy. Shortcomings discovered late in the process require backtracking or accepting the inferior.

The term *minimum viable product* (MVP), popularized by Eric Ries in the book *The Lean Startup,* indicates the simplest possible model that can generate helpful feedback.

MINIMUM VIABLE PRODUCT =
The LEAST you can develop before meaningful testing is possible.

An MVP is a skeletal version of your project. It can be touched, heard, viewed, tasted, or smelled, and contains just enough detail to be evaluated. That typically requires:

• A rough overview demonstrating project scope.
• At least one preliminary example of each crucial aspect.

Operational is ideal, but not always necessary or practical. For example, rather than coding a functioning app, screen layouts that illuminate the desired look and features may suffice.

Seek critique early on, incorporate what you learn, and iterate, iterate, iterate.

CHALLENGE: **Develop an online course that attracts 1,500 subscribers.**

Locked in a basement for four months, Clever Trevor built his first online course.

Unfortunately, it didn't catch. The topic failed to resonate. Its few enrollees grumbled about problematic bugs. Making changes at this late point would require starting from scratch. So he writes it off as a "learning experience."

Now it's time to create product number two.

This time, Trevor commits to testing the concept as soon as possible. Asking, "What's the least I can build before soliciting feedback?" he arrives at the following:

1. Course SYLLABUS including a lesson-by-lesson overview
2. Detailed OUTLINE for one "class"
3. Three-minute VIDEO SEGMENT demonstrating content and style
4. One sample ASSIGNMENT

After completing this MVP, he organizes a focus group. Responses prove invaluable.

At this early point, the vision and structure can easily be adjusted with minimal headache or backtracking.

Making Multiple Models

We've established the value of quantity while brainstorming. The same holds true when prototyping. For starters, puzzlers learn from each attempt, applying takeaways to subsequent mock-ups. Second, various designs can compete for adoption, or the strongest elements may be synthesized. Finally, reviewers provide more perceptive feedback when contrasting alternate visions.

Multiple models clarify a hierarchy of user preferences.

The following storyboard demonstrates a possible process.

sketch 12

prototype top five

test/collect feedback

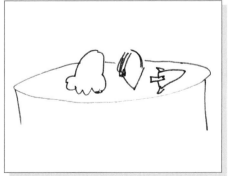

revise top three

second-round feedback

choose favorite & revise further

 To

PROPOSE

the remarkable,

ask great questions,
generate mountains
of possibility,
and prototype
the minimum.

CHAPTER 8

BLUE/BOOST & RED/RIP

Both BLUE/BOOST (positive) and RED/RIP (negative) feedback are critical for innovation. Weighing the psychological implications of these lenses, this chapter offers six critiquing techniques.

What works? What's wrong?

BLUE/BOOST & RED/RIP

There are two sides of feedback.

What works well? What needs to change?

Few puzzlers are equally comfortable with these complementary lenses.

Some love the celebration. Effusive with praise and enthusiasm, they spot good all around. Asked for suggestions, a meek response illuminates surface details at best. "Looks great!" is all they offer.

Others resemble Eeyore, Winnie-the-Pooh's insightful but cynical donkey friend. An acute ability to pinpoint shortcomings ensures that nothing emerges short of perfection. But with expectations so high, these critics have a hard time letting anything progress. After all, every idea can be improved.

Receptiveness to critique often depends as much on the receiver's disposition as the merit of the commentary. Some people generally write off compliments, assuming they are little more than superfluous lip service. Others are in constant need of hand-holding affirmation. Needless to say, feedback can be tricky.

Both boosting and ripping are critical. Innovation champions seek a balance.

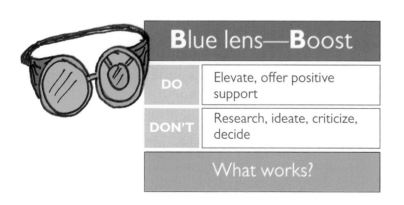

Blue lens—**B**oost		
DO	Elevate, offer positive support	
DON'T	Research, ideate, criticize, decide	
What works?		

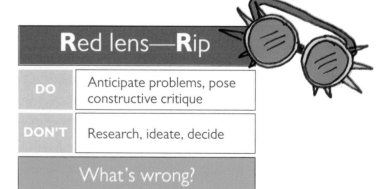

Red lens—**R**ip		
DO	Anticipate problems, pose constructive critique	
DON'T	Research, ideate, decide	
What's wrong?		

BLUE lens

Boosting with constructive praise offers:

Affirmation
Sincere, positive statements grow confidence.
Bravo. Efforts are paying off.

Emphasis
Affirmative messages stress what works.
Remember that. Keep that.

Construction Points
Compliments offer strengths to build upon.
This is good. Can you take it further?

RED lens

Ripping with constructive critique can be even more valuable. To benefit, however, puzzlers must be:

Receptive
Avoid feeling defensive or overly attached.

Perceptive
Able to grasp shortcomings and improvement paths.

Authorized
Possess capacity/resources to make the fix.

Blue lens

Boosting helps identify:
- Strengths & benefits
- Exciting properties
- Elements to maintain
- Aspects to amplify
- Ideas to build upon
- Assumptions that seem to be working
- Values that personally resonate

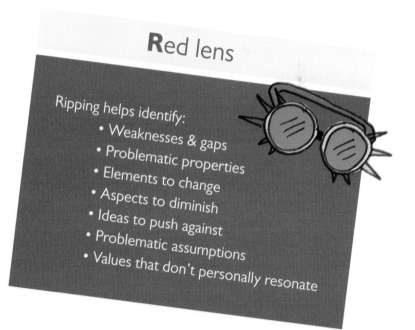

Red lens

Ripping helps identify:
- Weaknesses & gaps
- Problematic properties
- Elements to change
- Aspects to diminish
- Ideas to push against
- Problematic assumptions
- Values that don't personally resonate

The Challenge of Feedback

The new director, M. B. Shun, has big plans. He calls a full company meeting, introduces a vision, and solicits feedback.

"Following many years of business as usual, we now have an exciting opportunity to introduce this, that, and the other thing.

What do you think?"

I know what I think: *May Day! This is not going to go well!*

Even when the status quo clearly fails, most people are terrified of transformation. Ironically, it often seems the less happy people are, the deeper they dig in to protect a system they find offensive.

If change is on the menu, dissent and fear aren't just inevitable. They are appetizing. Welcome opposing perspectives rather than bottling them (until an explosion occurs). Anger builds when constituents feel shut out.

Concerns may illuminate important, otherwise hidden issues.

When RED lensing begins a change conversation, however, the well is poisoned. The mood is doomed before positivity receives a hearing.

Which brings us back to M. B.'s query, "What do you think?" With no clues on whether to boost or rip, control is relinquished. Unless the room is filled with quokkas (furry Australian marsupials famed for being the happiest creatures on Earth), negativity wins. Almost every time.

"The changes we dread may contain our salvation."
—Barbara Kingsolver, American novelist and poet

Feedback Considerations

Direction   Feedback can be pointed in three directions.

Project	*Past*	*Puzzlers*
Vet a **work-in-progress** with the goal of immediate improvement.	Reflect on your GAME or **previous experiences** to learn lessons for the future.	Comment on a **person's performance.**

Sequence   Architect the feedback arc with intention. The order of comments carries psychological and practical implications. By forecasting, "We identify strengths first, then turn attention to weaknesses," puzzlers know what to expect and can prepare accordingly.

Let processes—not whims—control the flow of feedback.

Big to Small
Articulate major issues before burrowing into specifics.

Small to Big
Address minor, easy tweaks before large-scale flaws.

Chronological
Start at the beginning and move forward sequentially.

Reverse Chronology
Start at the end (or with the goal) and work backward.

BLUE/RED combinations
Let GAME rules dictate boost/rip balance. Common processes:

All BLUE, then RED   BLUE—RED alternating   RED only
BLUE—RED—BLUE sandwiches   BLUE only   Random (flip a coin?)

Quantity

Each team and individual has a unique feedback threshold.

Few things feel better than a heartfelt pat on the back. A second compliment—and third—build confidence. But eventually, the *law of diminishing returns* kicks in. Excessive praise feels hollow or manipulative.

With some puzzlers, unwilling to overlook even the smallest flaw, suggestions emerge fast and furious. However, too much ripping is counterproductive, even when offered by true advocates. It overwhelms or triggers emotion, unleashing frustration that nothing is good enough. People tune out or give up.

LESS can mean more.

On the flip side, puzzlers fearful of confrontation or offending suppress true feelings and downplay concerns. Others avoid anything resembling a compliment, believing it superfluous. Yet meaningful critique and affirmation are necessary for growth.

Know your audience. Prioritize comments. Gauge their capacity when identifying the ideal quantity of feedback.

AND THIS, AND THIS, and WHAT IF YOU DID THIS!

Timing

Carefully consider the timing of feedback.

Premature critique thwarts creativity.

If we're just starting the experiment, micromanagement in pursuit of perfection kills the spirit.

Tardy commentary is frustrating.

When we've prototyped for weeks, yet you suggest major renovation 30 minutes before the pitch, don't expect gratitude. It's way too late!

The trick is giving just the right amount at just the right time.

Strive for a Goldilocks balance.

Language Polarity

Words communicating feedback can be as consequential as the message itself.

Negative vs. Positive

When used extensively, negative language is off-putting. Yet without realizing it, many of us regularly integrate this "tense."

Often beginning with the letter N, negative expressions include *no, nope, not, nobody, nowhere, negative, nothing, neither, never.* Other words: *Impossible. Despicable. Hated. Repulsed.*

And the biggest offender of all: "Can't."

It is possible for negative language to catalyze positive behavior: "Our city is in *crisis,* and we need you to act!"

But for best effect, use it sparingly. Creative wordcraft can transform negative statements into positive ones.

–		+
"No problem."	→	"Sounds great."
"Huge problem."	→	"Exciting puzzle/opportunity."
"Can't complain."	→	"If life were any better, I'd be you! (LOL)"
"I'm depressed."	→	"I need to reassess."
"This ideas sucks."	→	"This idea needs refinement."
"I don't like it."	→	"I prefer the other."
"We'll never get this done."	→	"Might this be simplified?"
"Stop eating that!"	→	"I know you love the so-called *heart attack burger,* though there's a lot of truth in advertising . . ."

Tip: NEVER place sensitive feedback in email or social media. Such negativity often returns to haunt.

You vs. I

The PRONOUN RULE:
BLUE = "YOU"
RED = "I"

Name away while boosting!
Sincere citations of colleague contributions offer validation and goodwill.

- "Building on Chen's idea . . ."
- "Burt's comment got me excited about . . ."
- "I love Margarita's point, and think we ought to take it further . . ."

Positive and personal is a winning combination.

Avoid "you" and "your" when ripping.
These accusatory terms feel like finger pointing, triggering resentment and pushback. Neutral or "I" language is preferable with the RED lens.

Rather than:		**Say:**
"Your idea is problematic." (Damning)	→	"This idea is problematic." (Matter-of-fact)
"Your research seems off . . ." (Dismissive)	→	"Can we double-check this research?" (Thorough)
"You made me mad when . . ." (Accusatory)	→	"I felt hurt when . . ." (Nobody can argue with the way "I" feel)

Neutralize critique.

Statement vs. Question

Suggestions can be declarations or inquiries.

Feedback STATEMENTS
provide unambiguous direction.
"This needs to be altered."
Feedback QUESTIONS
are more flexible,
unsealing the world of possibility.
"What if you tried something different here?"

Outcome vs. Solution

Feedback can:

1. Pinpoint an objective (outcome), or
2. Prescribe a fix (solution)

Consider which is most helpful for a given situation.

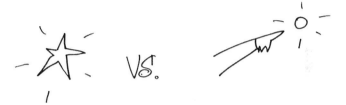

Outcome
Summoning exploration,
an array of options are invited.
"Let's bring more attention to this image."
Solution
Improvement is needed,
please make this change.
"Move that image down."

The best feedback pinpoints specifics.

"I love it!" isn't particularly helpful, and possibly suspect. Are you truly excited about the vision, or simply can't think of anything substantive to say? Whether boosting or ripping, support comments with particulars.

"I love the way your project does this: _____!"

Feedback for Humans

Team T has worked day and night developing a prototype. It's not yet perfect, but hits many success Criteria. Puzzlers are excited to run it by leadership.

Following a brief demonstration, the boss Noa Takt jumps in. "I see several problems. It's not up to code. This doohickey squeaks, and the color rubs me the wrong way." Darts fly until concerns have been exhausted. "Other than that, great job!"

Team T is crushed. Though Noa's comments are legitimate, was their model a complete bust?

Nothing could be further from the truth. Noa was impressed! But she doesn't waste time noting what already works. It's not her style. Unfortunately, this tactic blatantly discounts a fundamental reality.

Human beings are fragile under a microscope.

Even with a reservoir of trust (which Noa does not have), people crave validation. Before receiving critique, they need assurance that constructive commentary comes from a good place.

Noa's encounter could have gone differently. What if she pinpointed several features that worked well before offering "improvement opportunities"? Identical critique feels different in this context.

Brutally honest assessment is paramount. Never sugarcoat. But be sure to optimize the *sequence* of comments—and the mood in the room.

When offering or facilitating critique, consider the psychological trajectory. The closer someone is to an issue, the more sensitive she or he becomes.

Balance intent with how comments will likely be received.

"As a highly sensitive person, every little thing elicits a strong reaction in me."

—Tracy M. Kusmierz, American author of *9 Things I Wish People Knew About Me as a Highly Sensitive Introvert*

What Is Said vs. What Is Heard

RED and BLUE lenses are most likely to trigger emotion.

Some people thrive on critique, embracing its promise of insightful improvement. As a classically trained pianist shaped by decades of detail-oriented lessons, that certainly describes me. No amount of brutally honest dart throwing is likely to ruffle my feathers.

But not everyone shares this mindset. Some puzzlers interpret sharp feedback as a personal attack. They get distressed, defensive, or deflated.

The right comments meeting the wrong psychology do little good.

Though diverse teams are an asset during ideation, they complicate feedback. Commenters often harbor cultural biases, whether inadvertent or overt. Uneven power dynamics or rocky past experiences negatively influence how remarks are received.

This communication challenge occurs even in positive reflection.

Suppose Bill (a white man) begins critiquing DeAndre (an African American colleague) with an enthusiastic boost. "Excellent pitch. You are such an articulate presenter!" DeAndre is immediately offended, interpreting the message as a microaggression. "So you believe Black people are typically poor communicators?" he fumes.

Regardless of intent, one thing is certain. Any feedback from this point forward, no matter how astute or well-intended, is tarnished. Trust has been breached. The well is poisoned.

We all make mistakes. And it is impossible to accurately predict how every comment will be interpreted. An identical suggestion may be received differently by teammates or even the same person at another time. If your statement rubs someone the wrong way, apologize, listen empathetically, and learn from the experience.

Before verbalizing potentially harmful critique, consider potential consequences. Just "getting things off my chest" is rarely worth it in the long run. Ask yourself:

1. Is this feedback likely to trigger positive results?
2. Is this feedback likely to generate negative residual effects?

If the answer is "yes" to #1 and "no" to #2, go ahead. If not, consider another set of questions.

• Does it need TO BE SAID?
• Does it need to be said BY ME?
• Does it need to be said by me RIGHT NOW?

How to Receive Feedback

When on the receiving end of critique, your primary job is to listen. Take notes, ensuring nothing is forgotten; never rely on memory alone. Ask clarifying questions when helpful to fully comprehend each suggestion.

However, just as ideation should not be mixed with editorializing, feedback collection is no time for justification. Stay neutral and open. Never get defensive. Remember that idea critiques are not personal incursions.

Rebuttals are strictly forbidden.

Unless fixes are quick and easy, treat revision as a separate activity, to be completed later.

Not all suggestions warrant action. Consider which comments are most relevant.

Become a filter, not a sponge.

What Is Said vs. What Is Meant

Articulated recommendations occasionally imply more fundamental but unspoken root problems. Gain large-scale comprehension before embracing tweaks. Follow up as necessary to be certain you accurately grasp perceived shortcomings and why they matter.

What is the message-under-the-message?

For example, suppose a commenter suggests altering the curve of a chair you are designing. Rather than simple compliance, investigate further. "What about the current form doesn't work for you?" Perhaps the true issue is aesthetic, comfort, nostalgia, or something else altogether.

Sometimes small noted matters reveal foundational flaws that require drastic reimagination. The opposite can also be true—a major concern is adequately quelled with minor adjustment.

"Whatever anybody says or does, assume positive intent. You will be amazed at how your whole approach to a person or problem becomes very different."

—Indra Nooyi, Indian American business executive, former CEO of PepsiCo

Expressing Emotion

Puzzlers are scientists who must objectively follow facts, wherever they lead. This is not the time to inject personal fears or neuroses. Focus on the GAME.

But puzzlers are also human beings.

At times, life's weight is too much to ignore. Family emergencies, electrifying news, or the process itself can trigger emotional roller-coasters. While you don't want puzzlers to wear emotions on their sleeves, chugging along without acknowledging such sentiments can backfire as people disengage and check out.

It is occasionally necessary to survey the room. Doing so sends a message that teammates matter—not just as brains, but also as individuals.

"How do you feel?"

Common Excitements

Puzzlers get inspired when:

- Being part of something important
- Participating in the creative process
- Benefiting personally from a solution
- Helping an organization thrive
- Feeling listened to
- Collaborating in meaningful ways
- Building/strengthening relationships
- Experiencing the new
- Learning something interesting
- Contributing to success
- Encountering good news outside of the GAME

Common Disappointments

Puzzlers find frustration/fear in:

- Failure
- Losing control
- The unknown
- Pain or discomfort
- Unclear instructions
- New things/disruptive change
- Unintended/negative consequences
- Irrelevance
- Diminished personal importance
- The consequences of success
- Life outside the GAME

6 APPROACHES TO CRITIQUE

How feedback gets shared is almost as important as what is said. This section introduces six techniques.

> 1. SAGE Advice
> 2. Pointed Commentary
> 3. Report Card
> 4. "I Like. I Wish. I Wonder."
> 5. Fear Factor
> 6. Celebration Circle

1: SAGE Advice

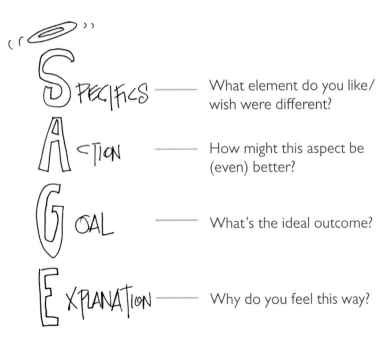

SPECIFICS —— What element do you like/ wish were different?

ACTION —— How might this aspect be (even) better?

GOAL —— What's the ideal outcome?

EXPLANATION —— Why do you feel this way?

CHALLENGE: Create a wildly successful workout app.

Cal S. Thenix hopes a new venture will change his career—and the world. With several established competitors, Cal knows his product must be user-friendly, flexible, and unique.

Early on, he invites a diverse focus group to review Prototype 1.0. Participants are encouraged to ignore surface details while zooming out to the big picture.

He requests SAGE advice, after explaining what that entails.

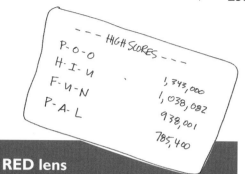

With SAGE advice, even positive observations lead to growth.
Cal finds inspiration in comments like the following.

BLUE lens	RED lens

SPECIFICS "I love how workouts are accompanied by videos demonstrating proper form."

ACTION "Even more helpful would be filming with a 360 camera."

GOAL "That way, users could zoom in and observe multiple angles."

EXPLANATION "I often feel uncertain about details— distance between feet, angle of wrists, etc. Give subscribers, rather than a cameraperson, control of where to look."

SPECIFICS "I wish the app displayed records of top performers."

ACTION "Might there be a leaderboard detailing achievements of similar users or friends?"

GOAL "This way, individuals can evaluate how their personal regimen compares."

EXPLANATION "I personally push myself harder when competing, rather than operating in a vacuum."

 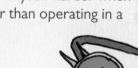

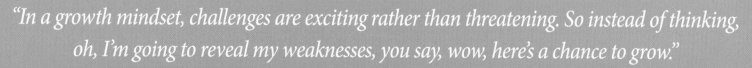

"In a growth mindset, challenges are exciting rather than threatening. So instead of thinking, oh, I'm going to reveal my weaknesses, you say, wow, here's a chance to grow."

—Carol Dweck, American psychologist, author of *Mindset*

2: Pointed Commentary

Once development is well underway, it becomes necessary to "proofread the project." Targeting small to medium glitches, suggestions are stated in succinct bullet points, avoiding lengthy explanation. Tackle larger, more complex issues separately.

 CHALLENGE: Create a wildly successful workout app.

Months and iterations later, the launch date approaches for Cal S. Thenix's workout app.

Summoning a new group of "critics," he requests a different flavor of feedback. Too late for major modification, the goal now is ensuring that everything works intuitively, without hiccups.

Zoom in and rip.

"Think of yourselves as plumbers, charged with spotting any weakness that could ultimately leak. No issue is too small, so be brutal. Identify as many flaws as possible."

Cal directs attention to details like:

- Typos and writing clarity
- Ease and logic of navigation
- Sequencing
- Content glitches
- Surface details like color preference

"The three individuals who offer the most RED lens feedback receive gift cards!"

As expected, there is redundancy between reviewers, and not every comment warrants action. But scores of valid issues are identified, many solved with a simple tweak.

Multiple critical eyes are invaluable.

3: Report Card

A report card helps evaluators focus their feedback.

Charge them with grading specific elements.

⭐ **CHALLENGE:** **Secure an investor.**

Business is booming at Weiner Brothers (WB), a hot dog joint that showcases Hollywood kitsch. To expand, however, they need capital.

Next week, WB has the rare opportunity to pitch to seven venture capitalists. With just one shot and terrifyingly high stakes, they invite 25 friends to evaluate a mock presentation.

Each attendee offers grades and comments on a "report card" listing a dozen critical aspects: value proposition, storytelling, business model, audience connection, charisma, slides, and so on. Scores from this large group provide a diversity of data, clarifying whether opinions are outliers or trends.

"When people tell you something doesn't work for them, they are almost always right. When they tell you exactly how to fix it, they are almost always wrong."

—Neil Gaiman, British author

4: "I Like. I Wish. I Wonder."

Requiring feedback to begin with a simple prescribed phrase can set the tone. For example, "I notice . . ." (GREEN lens) statements tend to be objective and nonemotional.

"I Like, I Wish, I Wonder," developed by Stanford's design school, is a powerful exercise for mining feedback and ideas. It is effective whether reflecting on the past or evaluating works-in-progress.

★ CHALLENGE:
Become known for having the best customer service in town.

Following several grievances from disgruntled shoppers, Shoe Shack manager Tim Burland-Bootz is determined to improve sales force engagement.

At first, he considers addressing recent complaints about employees head on. But that would place workers on the defensive. Instead, Tim gives them an assignment:

Go shopping as a customer experience detective.

While this research is a GREEN lens activity, they reflect afterward through a three-part feedback exercise.

STEP 1   "I like . . ."

Beginning each sentence with an affirmation, they isolate effective practices.

- "I like being greeted immediately upon entering."
- "I like affirming comments when trying on clothing."
- "I like when employees patiently answer questions."

STEP 2 — "I wish . . ."

After exhausting the likes, they turn to critique. Rather than negative language such as "I hated," even ripping has a positive spin.

- "I wish they'd escorted me to merchandise, rather than pointing in the general direction."
- "I wish some employees hovered less, while others were easier to track down."
- "I wish waiting in line weren't so boring."

STEP 3 — "I wonder . . ."

Finally, it's time to dream. What else might be possible? "I wonder . . ."?

- "I wonder if clerks might share cell numbers for easy tracking and communication."
- "I wonder what would happen if customers were notified when items of interest went on sale."
- "I wonder if purchases could enter you into a raffle for free meals with the staff."

During each step, Tim observes people nodding, actively processing how points might be integrated into Shoe Shack culture. When he discloses their ambitious challenge—to become local leaders in customer service—puzzlers feel inspired and empowered.

5: Fear Factor

With innovation the goal, fear becomes a common character. Rather than shutting it down, acknowledge and confront.

Following years of stability, everything is suddenly different. The new leadership team—led by someone named Evie Lution, nonetheless—is planning a major shift.

But change is hard. Change is scary. Just because it's necessary doesn't mean people will embrace change without a fight.

After hearing (mostly unfounded) grumblings through the grapevine, Evie gives voice to the resistance. One week before their annual retreat, she hangs a FearBoard in the lobby with the following question:

"What concerns you most as our organization transitions?"

Workers are invited to anonymously submit anxieties. Entries include everything from "getting fired" and "losing relevance" to minor, surface trepidations.

During the retreat, Evie quells many concerns and is transparent about others. She expresses gratitude for mentions that weren't on her radar.

Furthermore, she commits to hanging the FearBoard in her office as a regular reminder of employee sentiments.

And then the premise of their innovation GAME is unveiled . . .

 CHALLENGE: How might we transition, despite our fears?

Everyone feels calmer, heard, and appreciated. Maybe change won't be so bad after all.

6: Celebration Circle

When was the last time you heard unfiltered feedback detailing what people appreciate about you? Doing so is affirming and builds community.

Ray D'Ant's team project is about to launch, following several intense months. There is much to be proud of, despite challenges along the way.

Today's session, however, focuses on the community. Ray instructs his nine puzzlers to stand in a Celebration Circle. Here's how it works:

- Each person becomes a temporary "celebration hero."
- Moving clockwise, colleagues detail what is admirable about this protagonist. (Take as long as needed.)
- No negative words permitted; this is a purely BLUE lens exercise.
- Recipients must maintain direct eye contact and may not reply verbally. Just absorb the admiration.
- Once everybody has showered their compliments, move on to the next hero.

At first, Ray's team is apprehensive. "Is this truly the best use of time?"

Minutes in, however, their concerns melt away. Receiving sincere praise without responding is far from easy, but deeply meaningful. This day will be remembered.

Most participants are moved to tears.

Fortunately, Ray brought tissues.

■Your idea could be better!

Solicit meaningful feedback **(BOOSTS and RIPS)** and listen with hungry, objective openness.

CHAPTER 9

ORANGE/OWN

Puzzlers switch on the ORANGE/OWN lens when making decisions. After considering why it's so difficult to choose, this chapter introduces nine techniques for committing to one direction at the expense of many others.

What decision?

ORANGE/OWN

Perhaps you're a brainstorming machine. An ideation wizard. The floodgates of inspiration are wide open, as you drown in life's vast, infinite potential. But with so many options, which one is best?

In this vast universe, how can you possibly adopt a planet?

The inability to decide paralyzes teams and individuals alike. Fearful of neglecting even the most feeble solution, they attempt to be all things to everyone.

Others reliably secure safety. Finding comfort in familiarity that prolongs routine, they never rock the boat. Even advocates of incremental change may be subconsciously driven by compulsive fears of uncertainty and failure. The past wins

every time, with surface tweaks at best, even when the status quo clearly doesn't work.

Innovation champions, on the other hand, strategically choose their fate. Far from reckless gamblers, risk is minimized with thorough research and vetting. But in the end, they aren't afraid to OWN a future ripe with bold, decisive action.

Orange lens—Own

DO	Make a decision, commit
DON'T	Research, evaluate, ideate

Which choice?

The Hardest Choice of All

The hardest choice of all can be summed up in one word:

COMMITMENT.

Though loyalty is a virtue, it can be a tough pill to swallow even when selecting something spectacular, beautiful, exciting. Why? Because allegiance to one idea comes at the expense of a hundred others. Each decision triggers a thousand consequences.

Consider buying a house, taking a job, proposing marriage. Sure, your top prospect offers extraordinary strength. But it's not perfect. And there are so many other worthy contenders.

So you break out a ginormous stack of Post-its to BOOST (BLUE lens) and RIP (RED lens). "Here are the pros. Here are the cons. Consider the dream. Consider the rub."

Talking yourself in circles, you enter a state of near comatose.

No matter how profound or mundane the issue—shuffling an org chart, integrating new software, repositioning your desk—making choices can be tough. Here's a fact:

Every commitment comes at a cost.

As a result, in our era of unlimited variety and access, many people blow aimlessly in the wind. Wary of closing any door with promise, they stall and second-guess.

What Do You Stand For?

Standing for something is better than standing for nothing.

Or worse yet—*everything.*

★ CHALLENGE: What distinct values define our organization?

As a purpose-driven leader, Miss Shun recognizes a need for change. What her 52-year-old company does, and how they do it, looks a lot like the competition (only a little better or a little worse).

The process starts well. A change team brainstorms without fear, advancing 17 spectacular proposals.

Then it's time to ORANGE lens. "From this catalog, which three should we embrace?"

The group rebels. They aren't willing to choose. "All are beneficial!" puzzlers clamor. "Why would we deliberately ignore [X] or [Y]?"

But Shun knows better. "We cannot possibly do justice to so many values. In fact, close your eyes and recite them." Nobody confidently recalls more than five.

"If you aren't able to remember these now, consider how they will overwhelm our resources. Imagine if advertising asserted, 'Above all, we commit to these 17 priorities!' Nothing will stick."

Leadership requires saying "no" to good ideas.

"No 'yes.' Either 'HELL YEAH!' or 'no.'"
—Derek Sivers, American founder of CD Baby

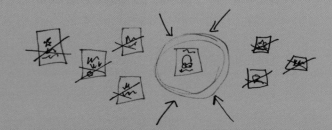

What Do You Stand For?

Some puzzlers resist ownership for fear of getting it wrong. But how consequential is a choice?

Treat the adoption of ideas like clothes shopping, as demonstrated in this storyboard.

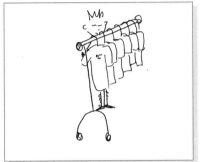

Browse Collection

Most Are Easily Eliminated

Take Several to Fitting Room

Each Gets a Chance

Most Make the NO Pile

Acquire One/A Few

Even purchases are "soft" commitments. Changing your mind for any reason triggers a no-questions-asked full refund. Returns don't indicate gross negligence or embarrassing lapses of judgment. Rather, they represent due diligence!

Make a choice—any choice—and test implications.

If it's ultimately not right, there is no shame in returning to the drawing board later.

Prohibiting Paralysis

Many puzzlers get caught in a cycle. Because no solution is perfect, endless debate prevents a leap of faith. Much is said, yet so little gets achieved. Stagnation, even paralysis, prevents progress.

Thoughtful deliberation is valuable to a point. But it is difficult to accurately predict obstacles and opportunities before jumping inside a puzzle.

Build and learn along the way, rather than pontificating until perfection miraculously appears.

Innovation GAMEs should mandate decision-making.

Whether selecting multiple finalists or a single champion, establish deadlines by which choices MUST be made, however imperfect.

Decide, test, fail, and try again.
BEATS
Debate, debate, and more debate.

Winning teams make decisions early on.

Doing so reserves ample time for future revision.

"It is very important to know who you are. To make decisions. To show who you are."

—Malala Yousafzai, Pakistani advocate for female education, Nobel laureate

Forbid the Safety Zone

Here's a common pattern: Fearless exploration, followed by retreat come time to choose.

Fresh approaches, even those with enormous potential, have a hard time competing against long-held biases. When stakes are high, timid puzzlers withdraw to safe, familiar territory.

To avoid this trap, mandate bold decision-making within the GAME.

Flip the List

After puzzlers identify predictable favorites, remove them from consideration.

Example: A marketing team prioritizes (a) social media, (b) print/radio ads, and (c) billboards. Taking these off limits, find inspiration through other, less obvious solutions.

Innovation Metrics

Include Guidelines with audacious parameters.

Example: A Constraint requires solutions adopted by less than 5 percent of competitors.

Jury Duty

Require teams to convince an external jury that their approach is big and bold.

Example: Pitching to five judges, each project competes for votes. Forty percent of the rubric evaluates "Level of Innovation."

Random Assignment

Require that some major decision(s) be left to fate, chosen by a picker.

Example: Rather than puzzlers selecting their project's primary audience, roll a die, shoot a dart, or pick a card to determine which option from a premade catalog is pursued.

The Decider

Who makes the call when it's time to decide? Not all rulings must be determined identically, but be clear about process early on rather than when controversy arises.

Approach	About	Pros	Cons
AUTOCRACY	Single authority figure makes important decisions.	Highly efficient. Leader may be most knowledgeable/ equipped to resolve.	Morale and buy-in often diminish. Proposals may be inadequately vetted.
ARISTOCRACY	"Ruling class" determines major judgments.	Benefits from multiple high-level perspectives. Each leader may be able to bring along own community.	Can still feel top down and create animosity. If majority of stakeholders disagree, a mutiny is possible.
OPEN EXECUTIVE	Big decisions by leader or a small group, informed by community input.	When there is significant trust on both sides, this approach can be efficient and well received.	When there isn't trust, suspicious stakeholders feel the arrangement is disingenuous.

Approach	About	Pros	Cons
DEMOCRACY PLURALITY = more votes than any other option MAJORITY = 50%+ SUPERMAJORITY = 60%+	Important judgments made by voting. One voice, one vote, regardless of status.	Winning idea has substantial support. Even dissenters understand they are in the minority.	Leaders may actually have better understanding than subordinates. Can be inefficient to build enough agreement. May result in logjam.
NEGOTIATION	Opposing factions reach compromise. Neutral facilitator must oversee.	May offer a balanced compromise. Each side gets something.	Waters down otherwise bold choices. Each side emerges disappointed.
CONSENSUS	Must have 100% agreement. Opposite of autocracy.	Exciting to garner unanimous approval. When it works, can generate great momentum and pride.	Even a lone dissenter halts progress. May be impossible to reach. Often time intensive.

9 Techniques to Choose From

Making sound decisions mustn't be a crapshoot. A number of techniques aid the process.

1. Priority Order	4. Purchase Power	7. Democratic Rule
2. Negative Selection	5. The BEST Idea	8. Random Selection
3. March Madness	6. Matrix Mapping	9. Juried Entry

1. Priority Order

An unambiguous pecking order emerges when you

Rank the winners.

With no ties permitted, prioritized lists show where each idea places.

While this technique is sometimes approached with intuition and unscientific personal preference, it is advisable to base decisions on some kind of benchmark.

For example, which proposal . . .

- Is most closely aligned with our mission?
- Is easiest to achieve?
- Is the lowest-hanging fruit?
- Is most likely to succeed?
- Makes the biggest impact?
- Generates the greatest return?
- Does the least damage?
- Is most unique?
- Is likely to generate attention?
- Will enhance reputation?
- Might lead to future opportunity?

"Instead of saying 'I don't have time,'
try saying 'it's not a priority,' and see how that feels."

—Laura Vanderkam, American writer and speaker

2: Negative Selection

When choosing a winner is simply too hard,

Eliminate the losers.

Even if you can't subtract to first place, clearing the field by disqualifying entries is a helpful step.

⭐**CHALLENGE: Introduce a beer that becomes our most popular.**

Drew's Brews, an up-and-coming microbrewery, is eager to shake up their menu. Following intense experimentation, the team agrees upon a secret recipe.

Now it's time to name this masterful creation.

PURPLE lens brainstorming generates a robust roster of contenders. BLUE lens nominations identify eight favorites—the group feels any of these would be great.

Unfortunately, come time to ORANGE lens, no consensus emerges. They are unable to decide.

Manager Bart Ender advocates a ritual of elimination. Going clockwise around the table, each puzzler systematically removes one entry from consideration.

Somehow, jettisoning individual items feels less painful than disqualifying seven runners-up at once.

Isabella:	~~"Hazy Summer"~~
Santiago:	~~"Whiplash IPA"~~
Bart:	~~"Whale Ale"~~
Evelyn:	~~"Any Porter in a Storm"~~
Ava:	~~"Hop To It"~~
Drew:	~~"Trout Stout that Makes You Shout"~~
Lakin:	~~"Fuzzy Novel"~~

And we have a winner!!!
THE WIDOW MAKER

3: March Madness

March Madness is an epic basketball tournament. Whittling down 60+ teams to a single national champion, round one involves some thirty games.

Victors advance; the defeated are eliminated.

Round two works similarly, but with half as many competitors. Each subsequent cycle reduces the pool further: Sweet 16, Elite Eight, Final Four, and ultimately National Champion.

The March Madness structure is also useful when ideas compete for adoption.

 CHALLENGE: Produce a viral video.

Hugh Jafans hopes his Country and Western cover band catches fire. With only enough funding for one over-the-top production, Hugh must decide which classic cover tune to record. The list currently stands at eight contenders.

1. Velcro Arms, *Teflon* Heart
2. I Ain't Sharin' *Sharon*
3. She Got the Ring and I Got the *Finger*
4. I'm the Only Hell *Mama* Ever Raised
5. You Can't Have Your *Kate* and Edith Too
6. I'm Just a *Bug* on the Windshield of Life
7. My Every Day Silver Is *Plastic*
8. *Bubba* Shot the Jukebox

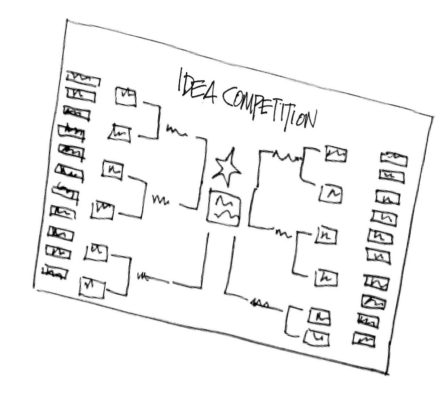

Using a March Madness approach, Hugh considers the relative merits of two choices at a time.

Teflon vs. **Sharon**   **Finger** vs. Mama

Kate vs. Bug   **Plastic** vs. Bubba

Next, the four semifinalists battle.

Sharon vs. **Finger**   Kate vs **Plastic**

Almost there . . . Hugh weighs the remaining titleholders.

Finger vs. Plastic

We have a champion!

4: Purchase Power

Things start to feel real when money—even pretend money—gets invested in ideas.

Bid on favorites.

 CHALLENGE: Radically reimagine one aspect of a car's interior.

Otto Moe Beal and his design team have an exciting opportunity.

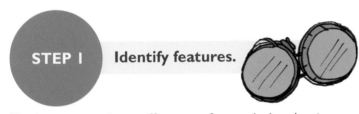

STEP 1   Identify features.

To determine where efforts are focused, they begin listing elements common to every vehicle (see Step 2).

STEP 2   "Purchase" favorites.

Rather than simply picking, Otto gauges relative interest. Distributing 20 Monopoly-like $5,000 bills—$100,000 total—the team may "invest" in up to five concepts. (He could have dispersed $5 bills, but larger feels more ambitious.) Results follow:

- Armrests
- Cup holders
- Dashboard—$25,000
- Doors
- Electrical system
- Floor mats
- Glove box—$10,000
- Handles
- Headrests—$35,000
- Key

- Mirrors
- Monitors/screens
- Pedals
- Radio panel—$25,000
- Seatbelts
- Shift knob
- Steering wheel—$5000
- Trunk interior
- Windows

$35,000 + $25,000 + $25,000 + $10,000 + $5,000 = **$100,000**

Unlike Prioritization, Purchase Power allows for ties. In this case, it also indicates an enthusiasm gap between the top three investments and final two.

5: The BEST Idea

When ranking on gut alone feels too arbitrary, score various criteria (from 1–10 or another scale).

Apply a concrete rubric.

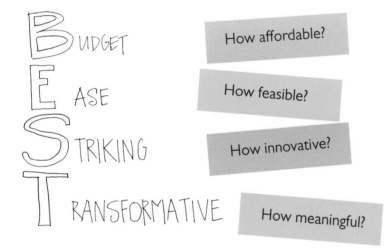

BUDGET — How affordable?

EASE — How feasible?

STRIKING — How innovative?

TRANSFORMATIVE — How meaningful?

★ **CHALLENGE: Introduce an exciting, experiential summer youth camp.**

Sommer Phun hopes to make a splash. After conceiving several concepts, it is time to choose and start planning. In truth, Sommer loves them all. Rather than just picking, a rating system determines the BEST (**B**udget, **E**ase, **S**triking, **T**ransformative) idea.

B — *Cheap = 10 - - - - - - - - - - - Expensive = 1*

E — *Simple = 10 - - - - - - - - - - - Difficult = 1*

S — *Groundbreaking = 10 - - - - - Oversaturated = 1*

T — *Life-changing = 10 - - - - - - - Insignificant = 1*

Concept	B	E	S	T	Total
Robotics	3	3	7	8	**21**
Quilting	7	9	5	6	**27**
Anti-Gravity Dancing	1	1	10	8	**20**
Tree House Building	4	5	8	8	**25**

Concept	B	E	S	T	Total
Zombie Fighting	9	7	5	2	**23**
Forest Survival Skills	6	8	6	9	**(29)**
Stunt Acting	2	2	9	6	**20**
Circus Performance	7	4	8	7	**26**

Looks like Sommer is headed to the great outdoors!

6: Matrix Mapping

Rather than ranking numerically, evaluate concepts spatially.

Demonstrate relative value with a matrix.

⭐ CHALLENGE: Which program(s) should we eliminate?

Manager Señor Sentar faces tough decisions. As his retirement home struggles, they must make cuts. It's hard to say goodbye to anything.

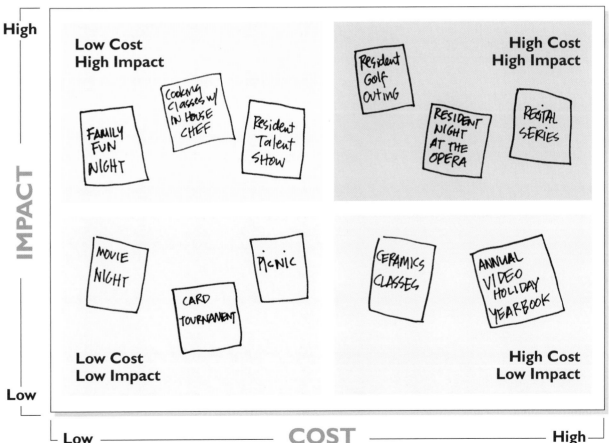

To help with objectivity, Sentar creates a matrix measuring cost and impact.

Each current initiative is written on a Post-it and placed in the appropriate quadrant.

Obviously, the best investments are low cost, high impact. But he hopes to keep items in the upper right and lower left boxes as well.

Two high-cost, low-impact programs—*ceramics classes* and the *annual video holiday yearbook*—reveal themselves.

They are first to see the chopping block.

7: Democractic Rule

Voting is a quantifiable, precise method for identifying communal priorities.

Let the people be heard.

Be clear about rules on the front end so participants don't feel the process is rigged or a moving target.

1. **Who votes?** Core puzzlers, everyone in the organization, audience/customers, etc.?
2. **How many votes?** One or several per person?
3. **What constitutes winning?** A plurality? Majority? Supermajority?
4. **How many victors?** A single champion or prioritized list of front runners?

METHOD	PROS/CONS	METHOD	PROS/CONS
Hands Raise hand for preference.	PRO: Quick. Dissenters see they are in the minority. CON: Peer pressure plays a role.	**Envelopes** Stick voting card/item in an "idea envelope."	PRO: Good system when lots of options are under consideration. CON: Congestion when many voters.
Applause Clap, hoot, or holler.	PRO: Fun activity that demonstrates enthusiasm. CON: Unscientific and imprecise.	**Post-its/Stickers** Place Post-it(s) or sticker(s) on surface of favorite(s).	PRO: A social exercise as well. See which concepts gain momentum. CON: Requires more time than a hand, ballot, or electronic vote.
Ballots Indicate preference on paper ballot.	PRO: People aren't likely to be swayed by the room. Counting votes and double-checking is easy. CON: Puzzlers can't see where colleagues stand (unless shared).	**Electronic** Vote through social media or voting app/site.	PRO: Better environmentally than paper. Tallied automatically and shared in real time. CON: Technology fails. Temptation to vote multiple times.

The time has come to plan.

CHALLENGE: Craft an ambitious five-year vision.

Senior vice president Em Powers believes voting on important decisions builds buy-in. To determine priorities and strategy, she organizes an innovation GAME, played by employees representing various levels and departments.

Throughout, multiple voting strategies are incorporated as proposals are developed.

Variety makes the process engaging.

At one point, puzzlers **spend a dot**, placing small stickers on favorite Post-it ideas.

Another time, she takes a quick tally of **raised hands**.

In a third instance, voting occurs through anonymous **paper ballots**, adding anticipation as preferences are read aloud.

Then, when determining a major companywide initiative, nine possibilities identified by the team are brought to an **independent executive council.** These leaders agree upon a trio of favorites and eliminate the others. Frankly, any of the three would be fantastic.

Because only one can prevail, Em collects input from across the organization. Her original idea involved an online poll, but she ultimately opts for something far more dramatic.

Five **poker chips** with the company's logo are dispensed to every employee, to be *placed in jars* representing the final contenders. An individual's tokens can support a single initiative, or they may be divided.

One proposal rises to the top, securing 18 percent more support than the closest competitor. Just as important,

Stakeholders feel grateful their input is valued.

8: Random Selection

The result of a world overflowing in abundant, dizzying possibility? Most people limit themselves. They order "the regular." They cling to *familiar*. The longer a catalog, the more likely safe choices emerge. To escape your comfort zone:

Leave fate to the gods.

 CHALLENGE: Arrange unique date itineraries.

Your Date Plus Your Date (YD+YD) is no ordinary matchmaking service. For a fixed price, they set you up and suggest what to do.

 STEP 1   Create a long, long list.

YD+YD has compiled a massive Post-it collection of 250+ activities within a two-hour driving radius.

From aqua aerobics to zorbing at the zoo, the roster contains scores of titillating options (nature bingo, clubbercizing, Frisbee golf, laundromat tours, panda feeding).

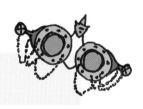

 **STEP 2   Choose randomly.**

YD+YD begins planning by selecting a core experience. Multiple methods leave things to chance.

- Throw ideas in air, see which lands closest
- Roll dice
- Spin a spinner
- "Idea raffle"
- Pick arbitrary number(s) and count
- Use an app/random number generator
- Pin the tail on the ~~donkey~~ idea
- Draw from a hat
- Throw a dart
- Spin, close eyes, point

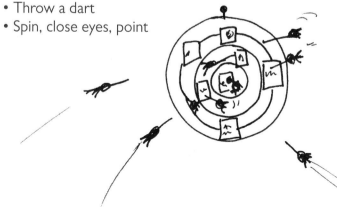

9: Juried Entry

Deep inside an innovation GAME, it's easy to proclaim loyalty where personal energy has been devoted.

External respondents bring less bias, more objectivity.

Most often, *Reveals* (competitions) are scheduled toward the end of a tournament. Judges can include organizational leaders, local experts, even users. After observing competing pitches or prototypes, they offer feedback and choose winners.

Whether prizes include seed funding, a green light to move forward, physical awards, or simple acknowledgment, good adjudication enhances the Experience.

> Also possible: Engage these authorities partway through the process to inform major decisions.

★ CHALLENGE: Introduce a compelling new college major.

Following a decline in enrollment, Heaven University's (HU) School of Public Health looks to revise its offerings.

A multiday GAME, where five faculty teams develop curricula, culminates in a public competition with an intriguing twist.

Prospective students serve as judges.

Interestingly, deliberation among adjudicators is forbidden. Rather than seeking consensus, each juror votes independently. They must answer:

"Which option would YOU pursue?"

After hearing pitches, asking questions, and weighing options, respondents have three minutes apiece to provide feedback.

Each judge then announces which degree they would choose. Interestingly, only two projects receive votes, providing HU clear guidance on which directions to pursue.

■ Standing for something beats standing for nothing (or worse yet, everything.)

Unapologetically **OWN** committed choices.

PART C
PLAYING TO WIN

Make your PEOPLE
—and your SOLUTIONS—
extraordinary.

PLAYING TO WIN
Part C Overview

Even flawlessly designed GAMEs cannot guarantee high-level innovation.

Teams often fall short of their potential due to weak leadership, infighting, competing priorities, or skill deficits.

A number of traps may be to blame. To increase the odds of success:

Level up your team.

Push them to try harder, work smarter, dig deeper, collaborate better, dream bigger. Provide the tools, instructions, and environment necessary to cultivate innovation champions. Part C is about leading puzzlers to victory.

Chapter 10

Facilitators are crucial characters within innovation GAMEs. FACILITATIONING describes the complexity of this position and offers 18 techniques to increase effectiveness.

Chapter 11

HAPPY TEAMS establish Team Tenets, mitigate Particularly Prickly Personalities, and cultivate conditions for Champion Collaboration.

Chapter 12

When good just isn't good enough, GETTING TO WOW suggests additional strategies for unlocking the remarkable.

CHAPTER 10

FACILITATIONING

Facilitators are crucial characters within innovation GAMEs.
FACILITATIONING describes the complexity of this position
and offers 18 techniques to increase effectiveness.

What does it take to lead?

FACILITATIONING

Innovation champions possess a secret weapon: *skillful facilitation*. The larger the group or dilemma, the more important this guide becomes.

Facilitation is a specialized skill, quite different from teaching, lecturing, or leading an organization. Yet there are few formal educational opportunities for cultivating these aptitudes. The best training is on the job.

Developing chops requires practice.

A facilitator need not be the CEO, department head, or other executive with a corner suite. Nor is a topic expert required—such authorities may be better placed in the trenches. In fact, it often makes sense to recruit a neutral, external voice.

Crucial, however, is appointing someone who relishes the gig. Though this job is complicated, the objective is not:

Lead your puzzlers to victory.

The Facilitation Gig

 Roles

There are several potential types of facilitation roles in innovation GAMEs. While skills and responsibilities overlap, each variety has a unique relationship to their puzzling community.

TEAM captain	Embedded member who leads their team throughout.
ROTATING captain	Multiple puzzlers share leadership role; play normally when "off duty" (*e.g., A, B, and C each facilitate one-third of the process*).
HYBRID captain	Figurehead who guides the process but is permitted to actively contribute simultaneously, like a normal puzzler.
GAME master	Neutral figure who leads a multiteam Experience from the "front of the room."

Be clear about which variety is involved, who plays the part, and what is expected.

"A leader is best when people barely know he exists. When the work is done, the aim fulfilled, they will say: We did it ourselves."

—Lao Tzu, ancient Chinese philosopher

Responsibilities

Part pilot, part conductor, part referee, facilitators must balance a variety of duties.

Part PILOT

The primary responsibility of a pilot is moving passengers safely from Point A to Point B. Though the destination and general path are predetermined, navigators make consequential decisions in the air.

Lives of passengers are literally in their hands.

Like a great pilot, the best facilitators:

1. Clearly understand the OBJECTIVE
2. Arrive with a MAP and plan
3. Comfortably LAUNCH the voyage
4. Pay close attention to the UNEXPECTED
5. CHANGE COURSE as needed
6. Project SAFETY, particularly during turbulence
7. Stay COMMITTED until the destination is reached

SAFE!

CLEAR ROUTE!

PREPARED!

Part CONDUCTOR

Orchestras project beautiful harmonies and complex counterpoint from every direction but one. Center stage stands a critical but silent partner. The conductor has perhaps the hardest job of all: consolidating the vision of talented, strong-minded individuals.

Aligning players, they procure unified and powerful art.

Like a great conductor, the best facilitators:

1. PREPARE for every session
2. Lead with CLARITY
3. Build CONSENSUS
4. Bring out the BEST in every player
5. MODEL behavior
6. LISTEN carefully
7. IMPROVISE when necessary

Part REFEREE

In a world obsessed with superhuman athletes, referees are oddly invisible. Yet without this arbitrator, games would collapse. Referees ensure that rules are obeyed, protocols followed, and time limits enforced. Critical when controversial calls must be made, perceived bias is unacceptable.

This professional must remain calm, neutral, and credible.

Like a great referee, the best facilitators:

1. Articulate/clarify RULES
2. Enforce TIME LIMITS and protocols
3. Keep the GAME on track
4. Play a consistently NEUTRAL role
5. Make CONTROVERSIAL calls
6. Are UNOBTRUSIVE, staying out of the way
7. NEVER RUN the ball (i.e., don't contribute ideas)

Balancing Act

An invitation to facilitate has Faye Cillie-Tater excited and nervous. The issue is tricky, and no progress has been made in years.

CHALLENGE: Facilitate well.

Determined to succeed, she turns the gig itself into a GAME.

Setting

CONSTRAINTS

is easy, since these elements were predetermined.

CHALLENGE	Given problem	
PUZZLERS	Assigned team	*cannot be changed*
PERIOD	Designated time	
PLACE	Scheduled venue	

Establishing success

CRITERIA

is a bigger riddle. What does "facilitate well" entail? Faye begins by considering *faux pas*. Certainly, she should NEVER:

- Wing it
- Waste people's time
- Talk too much
- Lose control or focus
- Micromanage

- Be dismissive/tone deaf
- Get defensive
- Contribute too many ideas/opinions
- Show stress
- Make it about herself

Though instructive, Faye would rather define success around positive behaviors. For example:

- Arrive organized
- Articulate with clarity
- Listen empathetically
- Create a safe space
- Stick to the schedule
- Lead the team to WOW

Faye is happier with this aspirational list. But upon reflection, she concedes "these points are all about *me*."

Then it hits her:

Nurture the

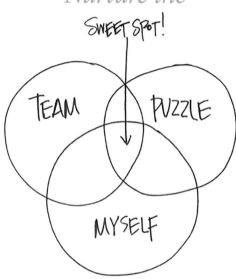

If focused disproportionately on the **team** and **myself,** THE PUZZLE may not get solved.

If focused disproportionately on the **puzzle** and **myself,** THE TEAM may rebel, burn out, or give up.

If focused disproportionately on the **puzzle** and **team,** MY EFFICACY diminishes, harming the entire process.

Facilitation is truly a balancing act.
Faye loves these goals, feeling her focus is finally on the right issues.

18 Facilitation Techniques

Seeking expert advice on leading a team, Faye Cillie-Tater (FCT) meets with legendary facilitator Grant Poobaw (GP).

GP: Faye, I'm delighted you reached out. So many facilitators just wing it without even considering strategy.

FCT: Thanks for sharing your facilitation secrets. I will be a stellar student!

GP: Spectacular. Let's get started.

1. Directing

GP: Facilitators must articulate UNAMBIGUOUS INSTRUCTIONS. What's the charge? Which lens? How long? Be crystal clear, allowing energy to center on puzzling rather than deciphering what the heck to do.

No matter how precise I've been, I consider it MY shortcoming when teams get confused. The larger the group, the more likely this becomes. If things get muddled, quickly reclaim the reins, providing alternative, simpler explanations.

FCT: What a great start! Today, I'm wearing the Green lens, hoping to learn 15 or so techniques.

Whatever you share, I will attempt to demonstrate in real time through my response. We don't have long, only a minute or so per point, so let me direct you next to lesson #2.

2. Absorbing

GP: The most important trait of a facilitator is ACTIVE LISTENING. Tuning out, even for a moment, causes problems. Accurately perceiving intentions—rather than what you'd like to hear—demands empathy, savvy interpretation, and reading between the lines. Sentiments that go unspoken may be at least as significant as those that are.

Direct eye contact and leaning in help connect while signaling engagement. Use neutral body language, showing neither approval or disapproval. Feel free to nod, indicating that words have been received.

FCT: *(Leaning in, nodding subtly, and processing.)* I'm hanging onto your every word. Tell me more.

3. Mirroring

GP: Mirroring refers to BODY LANGUAGE. Mimicking mannerisms or demeanor builds trust and rapport, particularly when it feels organic. Such actions send a message that you are clicking.

Perhaps you imitate a relaxed posture, talk comparably with your hands, or laugh alongside a conversation partner. Embracing jargon, verbal cues, or speaking style also builds connection. Just be sure not to copy negative patterns, like crossed arms.

(Opens a warm grin and raises eyebrows.) If someone trusts you enough, they may even begin mirroring from the other side. Know what I mean, ma'am?

FCT: *(Faye returns the smile and salutes.)* Aye aye, sir!

4. Scribing

GP: Spoken ideas are fleeting, easily forgotten or misconstrued. Only when NOTATED via paper or technology can concepts be studied, organized, edited, built upon, and reviewed.

As facilitator, ensure that contributions are adequately documented. You can perform or out-source this role. The best records incorporate as few words as possible but as many as necessary. Simple drawings/diagrams—alone or in combination with expressions—can be quite effective.

FCT: *(Faye notates the following.)*

 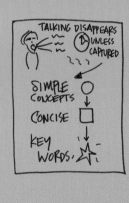

5. Clocking

GP: When facilitators lack a clear agenda, fail to enforce rules, or lose track of the clock, they often run out of time. Yet this gig requires meticulous TIME MANAGEMENT.

Establishing a relaxed vibe while making steady progress is no easy task! Take educated guesses about time needed per activity, and always leave buffers. During play, consider when to shave or add minutes. Train teams to work under the crunch of a stopwatch.

There are several more points when it comes to timing. For starters . . .

FCT: I'd love to hear them. But we still have many more techniques. Let's move on . . .

GP: *Touché!* You didn't fall for the trap.

6. Excavating

GP: FOLLOW-UP QUESTIONS, addressed to the contributor or full team, allow for deeper and wider exploration.

FCT: What kinds of questions are best?

GP: Common examples include:

- Can you tell us more?
- Why do you feel that way?
- Has anyone else experienced this?
- What other solutions come to mind?
- Is there another way to approach the issue?

FCT: Are there additional techniques that involve questioning?

GP: In fact, there is. It's called "boomeranging."

7. Boomeranging

GP: Team members often look to the facilitator for direction on tricky questions. But doling out advice can poison your position of neutrality. Instead of taking the bait, RETURN THE QUESTION.

Turn things back to the puzzlers. "How does the group feel about this?" When boomeranging, it can be helpful to add a point of clarification. "How might Thomas's research impact our thinking?"

Faye, what kind of approach would you like to consider next?

FCT: Hmm . . . What do YOU think makes most sense considering our focus on questions?

GP: Let's move to "sequencing."

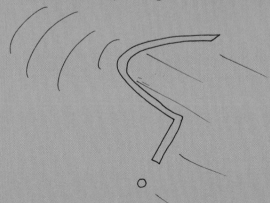

8. Sequencing

GP: When touching upon a hot topic, several people may be eager to chime in. But not everyone can talk at once. Flailing appendages do little more than distract and suppress active listening.

Acknowledge raised hands by establishing an ORDER OF COMMENTS. "First Johnny, then Maria, Bernice third."

FCT: This is hard to practice with just two of us. But next, I'd love to hear from . . . Grant!

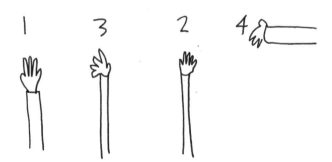

9. Recasting

GP: Even superb ideas may surface as convoluted statements, with unnecessary twists, superfluous details, run-on sentences, or insider jargon. Not everyone is skilled at speaking efficiently, and new thoughts formed in real time rarely emerge with poetic eloquence.

CONCISELY PARAPHRASED POINTS are more memorable and comprehensible than the original. See if there are ways to break things down that clarify and reinforce.

FCT: Got it . . . Restate what was said in plain language.

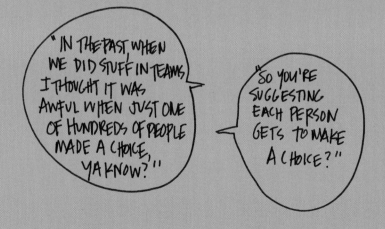

10. Replaying

GP: WORD-FOR-WORD REITERATIONS validate points, as if to suggest, "chew on this." When statements are made quietly, a confident repetition ensures everyone can hear.

FCT: *(Nodding.)* Hmm . . . A confident repetition ensures everyone can hear.

EVERYONE MAKES AT LEAST ONE CHOICE

EVERYONE MAKES AT LEAST ONE CHOICE !

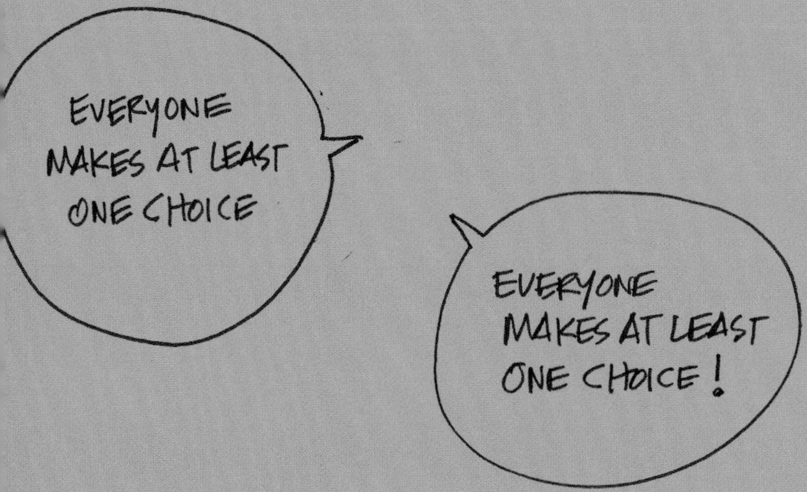

11. Stamping

GP: Stamping goes further, reducing what was said to ONE- or TWO-WORD LABELS. The ability to boil concepts down to their essence is invaluable.

FCT: Be *succinct!*

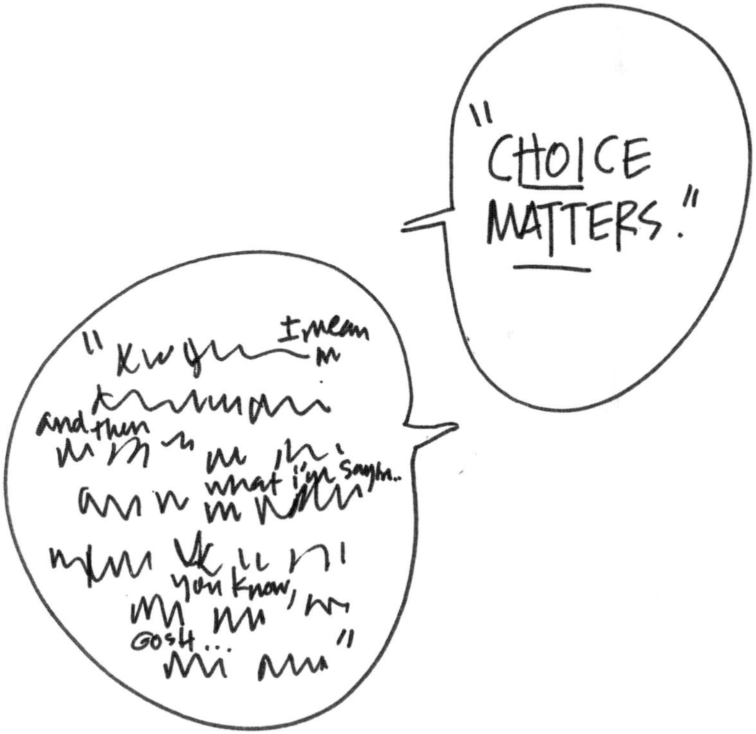

"CHOICE MATTERS."

12. Propelling

GP: GAME masters commonly circulate among multiple teams: absorbing, observing, taking mental notes. Occasional intervention is warranted to DRIVE TEAM THINKING. Some groups require clarifcation. Others benefit from validation—enthusiastic green lights.

Teams may need directed inspiration. Perhaps brainstorming is too limited, off target, bogged down in the weeds. Offer an intriguing question or prompt that catalyzes bolder, more focused thinking.

FCT: What if you introduce fresh constraints like a focus on technology, nontraditional collaboration, or other angles that direct the imagination?

GP: Excellent idea!

13. Harmonizing

GP: Because innovation requires making choices, one of your core challenges involves BUILDING CONSENSUS.

The key here is empowering everyone to feel appreciated and heard, even if they don't get their first choice. Whether the process involves voting, score cards, or other Orange lens techniques, emphasize that success belongs to the team.

FCT: I recommend we move to the next point. Does everyone concur? *(Grant nods his head.)*

14. Back Pocketing

GP: Some comments are intriguing but off target, suggesting a different direction or lens. Rather than taking an untimely detour or simply moving on, SAVE THEM FOR LATER.

Invite puzzlers to place these concepts "in the pocket." Draw an *idea pouch* somewhere, allowing proposals to reside there until the appropriate time.

Speaking of pouches, did I tell you my kangaroo story?

FCT: I'd love to hear about it, but let's not get side-tracked. Can we save this for later? (*Draws a simple "kangaroo" on a Post-it to place in the pocket.*)

15. Stealing Focus

GP: Even disciplined groups get sidetracked. Multiple conversations ensue, or brainstorming continues beyond the alarm. Quickly RECLAIM ATTENTION. Many options exist beyond shushing.

Sometimes, all it takes is a gesture. Move closer, farther away, stand, sit, subtly redirect. The Boy Scouts are known for two-finger peace signs.

Loud sounds—a whistle, cymbal, clap, singing—or flipping the lights are possible. Indicating "time's up," these actions signal attention should return to you. (*Grant elucidates for several more minutes, though time is running short.*)

FCT: (*Getting out of her chair and stretching.*) Great points, indeed. What else do you have?

16. Calling the Room

GP: At times, it is necessary to CHECK THE TEMPERATURE of your community. "Do you need a break?" "Is everyone on the same page?" "Are we working too hard?" Listen to feedback and adjust accordingly.

FCT: Everything OK, Grant? Do you bring this up because something is troubling you?

GP: Not at all. But it is an important technique.

FCT: Great, just wanted to be sure.

17. Futurecasting

GP: Some puzzlers grow impatient when they lack clarity about what's to come. FORETELLING even basic frameworks quells nerves and demonstrates a well-planned Experience. Sharing next steps also plants seeds, challenging members to think ahead.

FCT: Grant, you've been so helpful. I feel prepared to move to this book's next chapter. It's on team dynamics. There's even a section on Particularly Prickly Personalities!

GP: Wow, sounds interesting!

FCT: Before we run out of time, are there other approaches I should consider?

GP: Just one.

18. Recapping

GP: Toward the end of a phase or session, SUMMARIZE major points.

- Today, we accomplished . . .
- Some common themes were . . .
- Important decisions include . . .

FCT: It's been super helpful diving into so many techniques with you! To recap, it seems that facilitator roles are sorted into four major categories. *(Draws the following.)*

FOCUS	CLARITY	ENGAGEMENT	ADMINISTRATIVE
Directing Probing Boomeranging Back Pocketing Futurecasting	Recasting Replaying Stamping Recapping	Absorbing Mirroring Propelling Harmonizing Calling the Room	Scribing Clocking Sequencing Stealing Focus

GP: Excellent outline! I should also mention the value of inviting puzzlers to reflect on important takeaways. Beyond review, it illustrates what was retained. If their summary is incomplete, you can always fill in the blanks.

I think you're ready to lead! Good luck, Faye.

The higher the stakes, the more important **FACILITATION** becomes . . .

to navigate obstacles,
enforce rules,
and guide the process.

CHAPTER 11

HAPPY TEAMS

HAPPY TEAMS establish Team Tenets, mitigate Particularly Prickly Personalities, and cultivate conditions for Champion Collaboration.

What does it take to collaborate?

HAPPY TEAMS

Whether innovation centers on business or balance or budgets or bananas, one thing is certain. Human beings control your destiny.

Puzzlers are people.

Under the right conditions, people can achieve the extraordinary.

But they are a funny lot. They become high maintenance. They bring baggage. They get prickly.

While it's not possible to change human nature, much can be done to cultivate happy teams.

"Talent wins games, but teamwork and intelligence win championships."

—Michael Jordan, American basketball player and businessman

Team Tenets

Consider two overlapping GAMEs: your puzzle and your people.

Guidelines help solve the *Challenge.*
Tenets help solve the *Team.*

Turning collaboration into ART, strong Team Tenets inspire better problem solving. They become indispensable when complications arise (if enforced consistently).

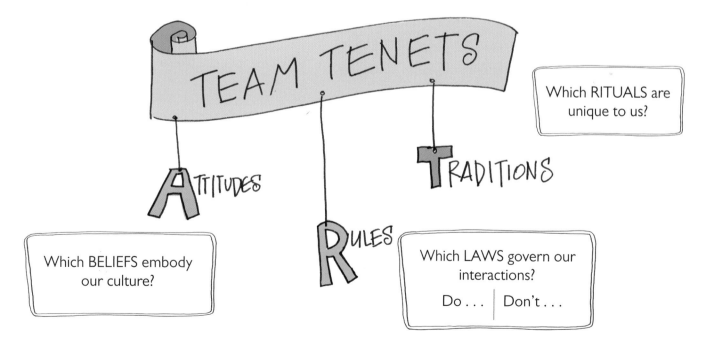

286

ATTITUDES: Which Beliefs Embody Our Culture?

The late Tony Hsieh, former CEO of the online shoe vendor Zappos, believed:

"IF YOU GET THE CULTURE RIGHT, EVERYTHING ELSE WILL FOLLOW NATURALLY."

More than mere words, Zappos's 10 "Family Core Values" are a way of life. They include:

1. Deliver WOW through service.
3. Create fun and a little weirdness.
8. Do more with less.

Notice, there is no mention of footwear.

Either you shape the culture or the culture shapes you.

Below are core Attitudes for my consulting firm, *The Puzzler Company.*

PUZZLER ATTITUDES

1. Almost every problem is solvable.

2. "We" is greater than "me" (and more fun!).

3. Embrace diversity through all we do.

4. Dreams first; then logistics.

5. Amplify curiosity and ambition.

6. Especially today, yesterday rarely describes tomorrow.

7. Find clues where no one else looks.

8. Seize opportunity in roadblocks.

9. Insist that positivity rises in parallel with difficulty.

10. Consider turning the puzzle over and discarding half the pieces.

RULES: Which Laws Govern Our Interactions?

Where attitudes are aspirational, Rules are tactical. They describe behaviors puzzlers should and must observe. Rules come in two flavors: *Dos* and *Don'ts*. Examples include:

Do . . .	Don't . . .
• Be punctual	• Check tech
• Be present	• Engage in side conversations
• Be participatory	• Interrupt
• Be pleasant	• Ramble
• Be positive	• Take it personally
• Be proactive	• Be prickly
• Be private (keep confidentiality)	• Hold a grudge

In addition to meeting protocols, rules can describe communication etiquette.

Do . . .

• Respond within 24 hours

• Label memos clearly (for easy sorting/findability)

• Make writing readable (concise paragraphs, no jargon, etc.)

Don't . . .

• Schedule meetings longer than 90 minutes without a break

• Include controversial, thorny issues in email

• Flood in-boxes with unnecessary messaging

TRADITIONS: Which Rituals Are Unique to Us?

What makes a team feel like a team, rather than a disunified collection of individuals?

Distinctive traditions build camaraderie.

This is why fraternities notoriously devise secret handshakes. Some customs evolve organically, while others stem from intention. The best examples are memorable and differentiated, offering positive flashbacks even decades down the road.

Cultural Traditions
refer to general conditions of play.

ATTIRE
Dress-down Friday; hat 'n' suspenders; purple pants; polka-dot socks; ugly ties

OBJECTS
Smurf-shaped crayons; bonsai trees; balloon purses; offensive coffee mugs

ACTIONS
Secret handshake; special knock; Secret Snowman program

Celebratory Traditions
unify the team when something goes right.

GESTURES
Snaps; silent applause; bird whistles; special salutes

SAYING
Insider phrase (one team celebrates by declaring "Coffee Kapow!")

ACTIONS
Group huddles; sing-alongs; fight songs; customized cheers

LOCATION
After big wins, visit a particular diner, bar, beach, tree, or other venue

Orchestrating ART

Team Tenets can be established in advance of a GAME or through a facilitated activity. Post this doctrine visibly. Incorporate refreshers as needed.

Be sure everyone agrees upon stated conditions.

⭐ CHALLENGE: Transform how we operate.

The radiant Hallie Looya has been tasked with leading a bold initiative for Big Company, a large organization renowned for its risk-averse culture.

Before even pondering solutions, Hallie must compel her team to buy into the notion of change.

Grasping the magnitude of this puzzle, she needs an ally in Team Tenets. Rather than implementing top-down expectations, their initial meeting centers on collaboratively defining priorities.

After distributing *Puzzler Company Attitudes* and *Zappos Family Core Values,* Hallie switches on the BLUE lens. "What resonates most?" Positivity emerges, with a lighthearted but productive discussion.

She then turns attention inward. "As you know, we've been charged with evolving our model. To prevent getting stuck, which Attitudes should we consider?" Puzzlers collectively propose 12 ideas.

Then it's time for praise, followed by concerns. Finally, they vote on five sanctioned beliefs.

The team seems pleased with these winners, and Hallie is delighted. If (OK, when . . .) resistance rears its ugly face, these mutually agreed-upon beliefs will become indispensable, providing clarity and guidance.

Rules of engagement require less time. Hallie asks puzzlers to suggest Dos and Don'ts.

After building both lists, she opens the floor for debate. Nobody chimes in. They adopt what is written.

Historically, Big Company's culture has been fairly sterile. Developing Traditions feels unfamiliar. One player pushes back: "Isn't that gimmicky?" Hallie asks him to trust the process.

She challenges the room to imagine meaningful and fun traditions. They become gradually more creative. Ultimately, the community endorses one *cultural* and one *celebratory* option. Unexpectedly, these customs quickly grow on the team.

Other employees notice a special bond among these puzzlers.

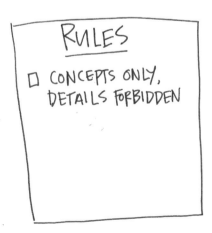

RULES

☐ CONCEPTS ONLY,
DETAILS FORBIDDEN

Their tenets, transcribed onto a poster, are placed prominently every time the group meets.

Big Company

Team Tenets

A ttitudes

1. Assume anything is possible
2. No sacred cows
3. Hold traditions lightly (rather than maintaining a death grip)
4. Grow!
5. Delight in all we do

R ules

DO

- Listen
- Wait before commenting
- Give 100% always
- Keep emotions at bay
- Smile

DON'T

- Judge before understanding
- Fear new things
- Get defensive
- Multitask
- Use tech in meetings

T raditions

CULTURAL	CELEBRATORY
Wear **silicone wristband** with *"assume anything is possible"* wording to all meetings	**"Wrist bumps"** (touch wristband to your teammate's)

Particularly Prickly Personalities

Human beings are intelligent, kind, clever, creative, collaborative, funny, and fragrant. We are also imperfect, complicated, neurotic, boneheaded, hypersensitive, awkward, and wholly insecure. Explained another way:

People can be prickly.

While Particularly Prickly Personalities make for great reality TV, they complicate the process of innovation. As a result, disproportionate energy must be spent managing relationships.

Address destructive behaviors head on, but realize that complete amelioration is not possible. Learn to accept—even embrace—endearing quirks of your teammates.

Do your best to ensure YOU aren't the prickly one!

When encountering prickliness, five approaches exist.

Option 1
Ignore

Sometimes it makes sense to just let things go. Accept imperfections and move on.

Option 2
Confront

Gently call out the behavior. However, public shaming rarely helps. The offender might shut down or initiate a private vendetta. Employ with care.

Option 3
Systematize

After diagnosing root causes, prescribe a remedy. A host of strategies follow.

Option 4
Privatize

Meet one-on-one to identify positive, workable solutions. Begin by validating, and listen empathetically. Perhaps a legitimate issue flies under your radar.

When appropriate, share concerns non-emotionally. "How can I support you while ensuring team success?"

Option 5
Eliminate

Some individuals are simply incompatible. They fight progress at every turn. The only sensible remedy may be cutting ties. However, consider this a last resort.

- You may not have authority to "fire."
- Even if you do, this act may burn a bridge, hurting more than it helps.
- It can have unintended consequences, destroying a safe space for the team.

Analyze the Issue

Three strands of prickliness exist:

TECHNIQUE-based
problem-solving skill deficiencies

PUZZLE-based
issue-specific fears or biases

PERSONALITY-based
individual idiosyncrasies

The pages that follow inventory common *genus* and *species* of prickliness. Each class is paired with an antidote and corresponding object.

Like Great Gaming Goggles (page 156), these articles are metaphorical. However, you may experience greater success by introducing strategies alongside actual physical items. Doing so is both fun and instructive.

Genus 1: Verbosis Maximus

May well have great ideas, but talks too much.

Idea.

Idea.

Idea.

Idea with details, talk, talk, talk, talk, explain, explain, explain, YAK, YAK, riff, lecture, *lengthy tangent*, endless story, down in the weeds trivia. OK, anyone else?

Once a RAMBLER starts, they hog the mic and kill the flow. Worse yet, a norm is suggested, signaling that others should equal or exceed this excruciating quotient.

Of course, there are times when deep explanation is necessary, even desirable. But proceed with caution. It's not common you hear, "I wish my colleagues talked much, much longer!"

Long-winded answers are a death knell for productivity.

Why do people talk too much?

- Soothed by their own voice
- Bogged down in the weeds
- Believe more words sound smarter
- Following suit after others gab
- Lacking skills to reduce ideas to the essence

Puzzler Antidote

SAND TIMER

Though functional tools, sand timers are just as effective symbolically. Hold it up as a visual stimulus, reminding puzzlers, "We want to hear from you, but quickly get to the essence!" Emphasize that *less is more*: A paragraph beats a page; five words are better than 10; two trumps five.

In fact, why not make it into a game? Offer a "concise messenger" prize.

Pictures are magnetic when framed with "white space." This principle translates to communication. People convey so much more when forced to say less!

BREVITY can be systematized by setting specific constraints.

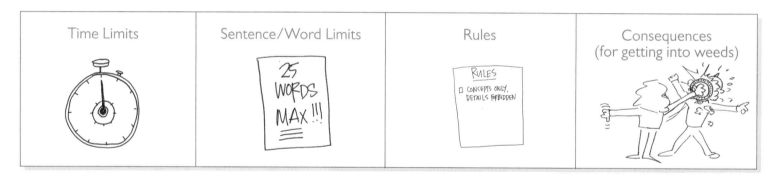

| Time Limits | Sentence/Word Limits | Rules | Consequences (for getting into weeds) |

"The most valuable of all talents is never using two words when one will do."

—Thomas Jefferson, third president of the United States

Genus 2: Quantitus Wrongimus

However, a failure to embrace quieter delegates comes at a cost. At least one-third of the population self-identifies as introverts. They can be indispensable.

Just about every team experiences participation inequity. EVER-READYS have an answer for everything, while MIMES find safety in the shadows.

Extroverts are often rewarded in teams and society. With an eagerness to step up, they are known for enthusiastic participation and dominating conversations.

Many introverts have changed history. Sir Isaac Newton discovered gravity. Rosa Parks refused to stand. Elon Musk explored space. J. K. Rowling brought wizards to life. Abraham Lincoln freed slaves. Dr. Seuss gave us a hatted cat.

Uneven participation isn't just problematic because *those poor quiet folks feel left out*. Overlooking human potential comes to the detriment of both your puzzle and your team.

Puzzler Antidote

POKER CHIPS

Every puzzler places three (five, etc.) poker chips in the left pocket. After each comment, one token is transferred to the right pocket. No contributions allowed after all have exited the original pouch. With this tactic, excited extroverts must think twice before jumping in. "Is it really worth spending capital on this?" Conversely, introverts are encouraged to step up and jump in.

Other small objects are just as effective: marbles, coins, paper clips, pebbles, coupons.

Additional tactics that help ensure all voices are heard:

Careful Management
Good facilitators balance discourse: "Who haven't we heard from yet?"

Systematized Inclusion
Rotate methodically until everyone has contributed.

Pass the Object
Pillow, balloon, Rubik's cube, or other article indicates who has the floor.

Small Groups
Equal participation is more likely in chamber settings.

Think-Pair-Share
(1) Work individually; (2) discuss with partner; (3) offer highlights to full group.

Social Media
Digital platforms can collect messages in real time.

Genus 3: Outta Focusus

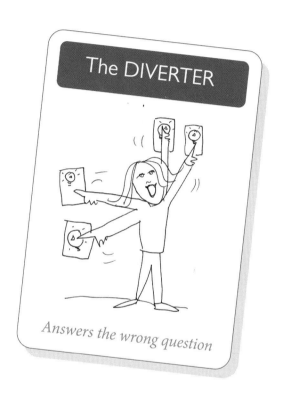

The DIVERTER

Answers the wrong question

The BEFUDDLED

Doesn't understand the question

DIVERTERS stall progress, suggesting solutions—even great ones—to the *wrong* problem. Or at least an issue that isn't currently under consideration.

Unskilled facilitators fall into the trap of chasing these beasts, investigating merits and demerits with an open mind. Jolting conversation off track, this tangent continues until another fascinating but peripherally related notion emerges. The cycle continues . . .

The BEFUDDLED are confused. They don't grasp what is expected, whether from unclear facilitation or momentary zoning. Rather than requesting clarification, they jump in and flail. The result falls on a spectrum between unfocused discourse and full-blown chaos.

Beware of puzzlers on the back of a frog, leaping nonlinearly from idea to idea.

Puzzler Antidote

PICTURE FRAME

When conversations veer off topic or exhibit confusion, take a timeout to regroup. Holding a picture frame, clearly reframe the prompt. This physical object emphasizes the need to focus.

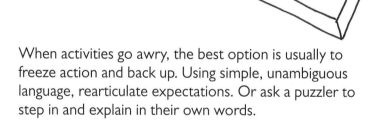

Facilitators are tasked with delivering crystal-clear instructions. At all times, puzzlers should understand the activity, lens, response time, and other pertinent PLANS (see page 129).

But things don't always click. The larger the group, the more likely somebody misses a point. When folks climb the wrong tree, you have four options:

1. CUT OFF the speaker and restate the frame.

2. ALLOW the comments, then refocus.

3. FOLLOW the detour to see where it leads.

4. BACK POCKET intriguing, off-topic concepts for future consideration.

When activities go awry, the best option is usually to freeze action and back up. Using simple, unambiguous language, rearticulate expectations. Or ask a puzzler to step in and explain in their own words.

Also keep in mind that most people are visual learners. Reinforce instructions with projected slides and/or printed worksheets.

Extra minutes for clarity trump time wasted in mayhem.

Genus 4: Ginormous Buzzkillus

A colleague in direct opposition to the team/GAME is particularly challenging. Multiple cynics reinforce one another. Their negative power can dominate even if representing just a fraction of voices. Unfortunately, this is all too common, particularly during change initiatives.

SABOTEURS are committed to tanking the GAME. Engaged and loud, they are first to arrive, leaving no chance that forward motion occurs without vehement opposition. Prone to negative language and a bleak outlook, Saboteurs hurl explosives on multiple fronts.

They exhibit defensiveness, bullying, even character assassination. When asked to BLUE lens, they simply can't imagine the positive, reverting instead to RED.

FEAR motivates saboteurs.

Fear their role will diminish, or require new focus, or become irrelevant. Fear of failure, losing control, evolution, uncertainty, the unknown. There may even be a fear of success. Whatever the root cause, Saboteurs are determined not to become accomplices to change.

APATHETICS, on the other hand, couldn't care less. Checked out and unimpressed, their prime disappointment is wasting time on your GAME.

Be careful not to diagnose Apathetics as Mimes. Though symptoms are similar, root causes are poles apart.

Puzzler Antidote

SUGAR CUBE

Turning things around requires a mutually resonating element. "Is there any intersection between project goals and your interests? Though we cannot change GAME Guidelines or Team Tenets, is there some sugar cube perk that might motivate positive engagement?

What will it take to bring you on board?"

Publicly calling out disbelievers accomplishes little more than exacerbation, triggering defensiveness or withdrawal. Instead, schedule a one-on-one meeting.

Begin by taking the pulse. "In your opinion, what is and isn't going well?" Resist the urge to comment. Instead, listen empathetically. Seek root causes of the resistance/passivity. Validate by signaling, "I'm listening and hear your concerns."

After providing ample opportunity for the detractor to comment, calmly share some tough love.

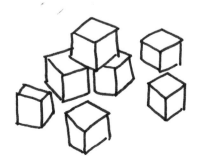

"We are charged with solving *this puzzle* for *this reason.* Yet it feels our team is working at cross-purposes. *Though we can't jeopardize the mission,* I sincerely value you. Considering the hand we've been dealt, let's explore win-win solutions. I may not be able to implement all—even any—of your proposals, but promise to give them full consideration."

Notice a few things about this exchange:

- It begins with listening.
- Dissent is welcome. (Allowing concerns to be expressed may be enough to diffuse tension.)
- The word YOU is never used accusingly, as in "you did this . . ."
- It states that although the puzzle itself cannot be compromised, you and your perspectives are valued.
- The prickly partner is invited to suggest solutions, though authority remains with the leader.

Genus 5: Egotisticus Majora

The SELF-PROCLAIMED PRODIGY

Knows it all

The PRIMA DONNA

Knows it's all about them

The BAGGAGE HANDLER

Knows it already

SELF-PROCLAIMED PRODIGIES genuinely believe they are experts on every topic. As indispensable superheroes, the entire effort would surely flop without them.

Being the smartest in the room, they rarely concede points or are willing to compromise. Great clairvoyance makes such settlements unnecessary.

Words often carry a whiff of condescension.

PRIMA DONNAS talk as if they are the center of the universe, regardless of project, problem, or conversation.

Pushing back against anything that diminishes their gravity, they rarely build on ideas of others. Self-impressed insights include MY idea, MY theory, MY experience, MY education, MY hope.

Some *narcissists* look aggressively down upon colleagues. Others simply don't notice anyone else.

BAGGAGE HANDLERS previously addressed this problem. As a result, reimagination is met with resistance, even when pivoting feels beneficial to others.

Regularly citing the past solution, they are convinced of its divinity. Unless—of course—previous efforts landed in stalemate, in which case failure feels imminent.

Acute with folks who generated the idea, concepts near and dear to the heart commonly trigger "Founder's Syndrome."

Puzzler Antidote

MAGNET

Magnets have two distinct sides: a north pole that attracts energy and a south pole that repels it. To cultivate team cohesion, require that polarity draws energy from the room rather than the speaker. A statement might begin, "Building on Marty's idea . . ." While this tool won't transform deep personality flaws, it does systematize the celebration of teammates.

Egocentric tendencies grow in some people for a variety of reasons: childhood neglect, personal insecurity, fragile self-esteem, genetic imbalance, years of playing the big fish in a tiny pond. It is unrealistic to believe that simple puzzling measures will override a lifetime of programming. That requires psychotherapy.

However, consistent rules and actively managed activities can help. For example:

- **We over Me.** First person words like "me," "my," and "I" are banned.

- **Getting Buzz-ted.** Facilitator hits a buzzer when self-references or past experiences are cited, reinforcing WE over ME in a lighthearted, gamelike manner (rather than punitively).

- **Pass it on.** Puzzlers may ONLY share ideas emanating from others—who they name out loud.

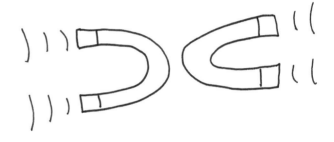

- **Role-play.** Puzzlers take on roles of relevant "characters," rather than responding as themselves.

- **Delegation.** Assign afflicted puzzlers to duties like scribing, timing, etc. (less likely to disrupt).

Above all, emphasize we're all in this together!

Success belongs to the team.

Champion Collaboration

Everyone gets prickly from time to time. Being able to spot, diagnose, and treat symptoms goes a long way. But mitigating these quirks is not enough.

Truly happy teams require something else.

The most successful communities optimize:

1. **C**onditions
2. **C**larity
3. **C**ulture
4. **C**onsensus
5. **C**ompletion

Conditions:
Optimize the Environment

In the theater world, bad lighting ruins everything. Great illumination, on the other hand, goes unnoticed.

Similar principles apply to puzzling. You're on the right track if participants barely mention logistics beyond occasional "well-oiled machine" references. Luxury isn't necessary. Just offer comfort and eliminate annoyances.

Distractions	Preparation	Scheduling	Seating
disruptions minimized	thoughtful agenda set in advance	ample time for work, engagement, & breaks	comfortable chairs

Sight	Snacks	Sound	Space
easily visible presenters, projections, etc.	appropriate refreshments and drinks	speaking/playback clearly audible	enough room to comfortably maneuver

Supplies	Technology	Temperature	Vibe
materials readily available	projection/tech works smoothly	not too hot or cold	calm, welcoming atmosphere

Clarity:
Stamp Out Ambiguity

Problem solving is hard.

Make comprehension a breeze.

The Experience must be carefully planned and orchestrated. Puzzlers should struggle with solutions, not purpose; assignments, not instructions; fulfilling responsibilities, not guessing who does what.

Facilitators should be trained, comfortable with the process, and able to articulate directives with eloquence.

Culture:
Empower the Team

Well-designed GAMEs are seductive. Their magnetism attracts contributors IF the culture is right. High-level commitment is most likely when puzzlers feel:

Authorized
Bestowed with permission and power to offer consequential input

Autonomous
Able to contribute without fear of micromanagement

Accountable
Held to task for achieving results

Appreciated
Valued, listened to, never taken for granted

Ambitious
Challenging (but solvable) puzzles generate more excitement than superficial, simple ones

"Clarify what you are for, not against. This is true power."

—Annie Zalezsak, Canadian author

Consensus:
Foster Compromising Spirit

Differences of opinion are sure to arise. Occasional friction and wrangling-before-compromise become experiential hallmarks. Such spirited debate isn't merely permissible. It's healthy.

But ultimately, puzzlers may need to compromise, willingly sacrificing personal preference in the name of the greater good. Imperfect solutions are better than logjams.

Happy teams find ways to come together.

Completion:
Get It Done!

How many individuals, teams, and organizations maintain an ever-expanding collection of incomplete projects? Quick to dive into any puzzle pool that whets (wets?) the appetite, each effort begins with a splash. Over time, however, commitment diminishes. Bored or distracted, they move to that next big thing—before reaching the other side.

Exploration, experimentation, and cherishing the journey can be their own reward. However,

To win big, you must deliver, ship, score, reach "THE END."

Most *Puzzler Company* GAMEs involve deliberately diverse teams. Beyond mirroring the kind of rich world in which so many of us aspire to live, this priority amplifies innovative potential.

But such a framework also introduces challenges. Even committed, caring puzzlers carry implicit bias, emotional triggers, personal baggage, faulty assumptions. Collisions may erupt, blocking progress or goodwill. Left unaddressed, a team will likely fail and depart disheartened.

During long GAMEs, we regularly employ a trained *wellness ambassador* whose primary role is addressing interpersonal and intrapersonal ailments. Rather than running from the risk of conflict, we treat it as a growth opportunity. In our experience, this approach yields a positive endame almost every time, despite inevitable bumps along the way.

In fact, gamification is a great strategy for making organizational culture more inclusive, even when the stated challenge addresses something else altogether.

■ HAPPY TEAM

doesn't mean
conflict free.

It does require respect, common purpose, and crossing a finish line . . . . *together.*

CHAPTER **12**

GETTING TO WOW

When *good* just isn't good enough, GETTING TO WOW
suggests additional strategies for unlocking the remarkable.

What does it take to win?

GETTING TO WOW

The concept feels right. Puzzlers are ecstatic. But it's tough to be objective about your own creation. Does it pass the test of scrutiny? Will people care?

Is it truly innovative?

There's a quick way to find out. Convene a group of trustworthy outsiders who bring fresh eyes and ears. Succinctly pitch your vision and invite brutally honest feedback. Rather than elaborate commentary, however, request one of three simple reactions.

MEH . . .	HMM ???	WOW !!!
"Doesn't do it for me . . ."	*"Has potential, tell me more ? ? ?"*	*"This is mind-blowing ! ! !"*

A single word—just three letters—speaks volumes. Consistent scores of MEH or HMM mean additional work may be required. Follow up as needed.

Innovation champions play to win. When *good* just isn't good enough, here are some final strategies for unlocking the remarkable. The results?

WOW ! ! !

Dreams First

Your idea sounds lovely, but let's face it—we cannot afford that. The boss will say no. There's not enough time, too much bureaucracy, and zero chance we have the resources.

Let's get practical!

And thus the dreambird is fatally maimed before even leaving its nest.

Many people lose their ability to think BIG.

Years of standardized testing and prescriptive job requirements convert them into risk-averse idea police. Litmus tests weigh any chance for failure, rather than potential paths to success.

In reality, just about any puzzle is solvable with enough grit and creativity. Remarkably, humans invented electricity and reached the moon. They are likely capable of decoding your puzzle as well.

To get to WOW, take pragmatism off the table, at least initially. Reach for the constellations. Embrace Puzzler Attitude #3 (page 286):

Dreams first; then logistics.

There will be plenty of time to reel things back to hardheaded realism. But at the start, reserve ample time for exploration and wonder.

"Never limit yourself because of others' limited imagination.
Never limit others because of your own limited imagination."

—Mae Jemison, American astronaut, first Black woman to travel into space

Best in the World

What does it take to become the best in the world?

Any serious athlete, musician, or dancer knows the secret:

PRACTICE!

Yet does this conventional wisdom survive the test of scrutiny? Even if devoting 23 hours per day for the next 59 years, do YOU truly have what it takes? And is this advice equally applicable to organizations?

For most mere mortals, the answer is a resounding "no!" As a result, we downgrade ambition. Accepting "better" or "very good" as the destination, attention turns to metrics ubiquitous across our domain. For musicians, the default is practice. For cleaners, it is laundering.

Puzzlers further rig the game, shrinking the meaning of "world." Rather than stretching ambition, they diminish scope. "How might we become *one* of the best in the world . . . among mid-sized-low-elevation-Southeastern-capital-cities-starting-with-the-letter-J?"

Success is undoubtedly possible without a best-in-class trophy. However, imagine the benefits such esteem would bring: more demand, more buzz, more clients, more impact.

Opportunities would fall into your lap.

You don't have to be a world champion . . .

But it sure wouldn't hurt!

Enough with the modesty and shrunken dreams! Instead, what if you ask:

"With my/our unique background, skills, and interests, what might I/we do better than anyone else?"

Reframing the question changes everything. Suddenly YOU, rather than competition or historic precedent, move to the driver's seat.

From this perspective, how might you become a "world leader" (whatever that means)?

Proficiency

I'm an unapologetic advocate of excellence. But doing what everyone else does (only slightly better or worse) is a tough haul. In a world bursting with talent, few of us become this kind of global champ.

You probably can't out-Harvard Harvard.

Furthermore, even if you do, rewards may not be commensurate. Superior quality does not guarantee notoriety. Yes, *please* strive for the highest quality. Never accept mediocrity.

But realize this alone may not be enough. For better or worse, many other factors influence success.

Extreme Differentiation

Highly distinctive features are easier to explain and more often appreciated.

Suppose *Something Extra Taxis* safely delivers clients to designated addresses. That just ties the competition. In contrast, "The only transportation company to offer free cookies and cocoa" instantly highlights a unique, uncontested value.

Fill a gap, turn left, do the opposite.

Shrink, Then Explode

First narrow focus. This might mean serving a specific audience (magic for lawyers) or expertise (chairs featuring penguin carvings).

Then blow up every square inch of that space. Suppose you become the world's leading portobello chef. Master every cuisine integrating this special ingredient. Open a fungi stand. Book *Alice in Wonderland* tours. Start a blog. Film a documentary. Found a holiday.

Define your niche and own it.

Fresh Combination

Remarkable performance is oddly . . . *unremarkable*. A lot of people and organizations do one thing well.

Yet we are fascinated by multitalents.

That's why music videos are more likely to go viral with one person on five instruments over five artists playing one apiece . . . even if audio is identical.

Unusual mashups are harder to imitate and easy to recognize. Package multiple talents (basketball player who rollerskates), services with causes (realtor committed to ending homelessness), or unique collaborations (barbershop showcasing acrobatics).

Uncommon Exposure

It is difficult for a book on dogs to attract attention in a bookstore carrying tens of thousands of titles. It's far easier in a pet shop displaying just this one text.

Apply for grants, market products, display your value in the WRONG places. Claiming the mantle of "best" is easier when in a class of your own.

Be seen where nobody else is like you.

 Negative Mission

In theory, *mission statements* describe the unique purpose of a person, organization, or project. In reality, the vast majority use flowery mumbo jumbo that is neither distinctive nor substantiated. If 10 direct competitors were presented with these proclamations (names blotted out), most stakeholders would be hard-pressed to identify their own tribe.

Negative mission statements present a powerful alternative. This two-part declaration identifies a traditional aspect you reject and what occurs in its place (thanks to freed resources). For example, if you designed a supermarket with no carts or cash registers, what would occur instead? When aspects taken for granted are deemed off-limits, unconventional thinking follows.

Of course, shaving off just a fraction of something may be enough to unlock exciting new possibilities.

_____ commits to NOT _____ . Instead, _____ .

(project/org name)   (something competitors do)   (something unique to us)

CHALLENGE: Amplify the impact of our symposium.

Social Problems Action Meeting (SPAM) is planning their annual conference.

Like most such events, they have traditionally featured lectures, almost exclusively. While messages are consistently inspiring, May Kadif-Rense suspects another format could be more meaningful. Drafting a negative vision statement helps them recognize new opportunity.

SPAM commits to NOT scheduling lecture-dominated symposiums.

INSTEAD, 75 percent of sessions will feature team-based GAMEs addressing real-world problems.

Stretching Up

"Reach as high as you can," I challenged the audience. They strained to grab the sky. The next request?

"Reach even higher."

Remarkably, everyone did. They climbed on tiptoes, chairs, tables, one another.

Which begs the question: *Why so much failure the first round?* Was it lack of ambition, or imagination?

A similar phenomenon happens regularly with puzzlers, particularly those new to innovation. Though invested in a colorful process, their hard work turns up shades of gray. Proposals are certainly not milquetoast, but closer to HMM . . . than WOW ! ! !

"Always remember, you have within you the strength, the patience, and the passion to reach for the stars to change the world."

—Harriet Tubman, American abolitionist

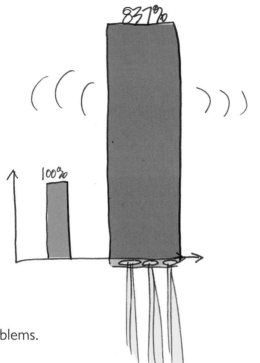

Most people and teams pursue MINIMUM success requirements. They work hard, aiming to reach widely accepted benchmarks.

- An organization does its work adequately.
- A student strives for the A.
- A jigsaw club fits pieces together.

But why stop there? Innovation champions set a higher bar. Jetting past the criteria, they combine bold vision with tenacious ambition.

- An organization far exceeds quotas.
- A student transforms assignments into an entrepreneurial venture.
- The jigsawyers publish op-eds, applying puzzle strategies to societal problems.

Blow away the competition by every metric.

Just about every idea can be improved.

The atmosphere above holds vast potential, begging to be discovered. After committing to a solution, add a sprinkle more magic. Using techniques from this book or beyond, strive for the next level. Challenge puzzlers to stretch up before ending your GAME.

One. Final. Time.

Puzzlers are capable of achieving extraordinary problem solving—innovation—when challenged to do so.

Powerhouse Proposals

While innovation comes in many packages, here's a winning formula:

1 BIG Idea **+** **3** WOWables **+** *a litle something extra* **=** **1** *Powerhouse Proposal*

BIG Idea

Despite intriguing features, many otherwise promising proposals fail to inspire. They offer too much content, too little to hold onto. The concept just isn't *sticky*.

Powerhouse pitches showcase a memorable hook.

At the heart of every WOW proposal is a BIG Idea. To qualify, it must be:

SINGULAR	SIMPLE	SURPRISING	STRESSED
One clear umbrella concept	Easy to comprehend	Unusual, intriguing, remarkable	Consistently repeated

This book is chock-full of innovation strategies: crafting guidelines, assembling materials, designing processes, proposing solutions, supplying feedback. I could talk for days on end about the methodology (just ask my wife).

But every feature supports a single BIG Idea:

Turn problems into GAMEs— and play to win!

WOWables

Major innovations are typically introduced as second-level items. Each should squarely align with the BIG IDEA rather than compete against it. To earn the title of WOWable, a pinch of spectacular is required.

WOWables take your breath away.

Not everything can WOW, nor does it need to. Plenty of HMMables, even MEHables, shape our lives. Even revolutionary inventions integrate programmatically sound—yet hardly mind-blowing—aspects.

That said, if the goal is to dazzle, design at least *one* feature worthy of this coveted designation. To win big, develop three.

BIG Idea X incorporates a trio of WOWables:
(1) this (WOW!), (2) that (WOW!),
and (3) the other thing (super WOW!).

If you discover a solution that's adequate but fails to awe, consider how much reimagination is necessary.

Lonely Bluff (LB) City Council hopes to dramatically increase traffic around their sleepy commercial area.

 CHALLENGE: Transform our shopping district into an in-demand destination.

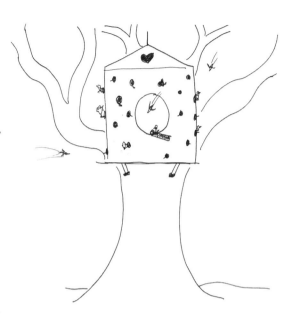

Prepared to invest $100,000, they organize a multiday innovation GAME involving 100+ neighbors. During the culminating tournament, 12 teams pitch. Collectively, a wealth of suggestions emerge: more trees, improved parking, public art, a new café.

But one proposal stands apart. Built around a poignant, unexpected hook, the winning team unveils three stunning features, each more exciting than the last.

The BIG IDEA	Our concept is summed up in one word: BIRDHOUSES!
WOWable #1	Shopping district streets will be lined with birdhouses decorated by LB families. Displays are entered into a competition with several categories: beautiful design, innovative approach, powerful story. Visitors view this public art and vote on favorites over the course of a month.
WOWable #2	The awards ceremony features local celebrities, a high school marching band, video montages of finalists, and $10,000 in prizes. During an extravagant finale, 100 doves are released into the air.
WOWable #3	The *pièce de résistance?* A giant, human-sized birdhouse playground, perched high in a tree, featuring ziplines that deliver passengers to local stores.

Judges come to quick consensus: WOW ! ! !

A Little Something Extra

What's the key to unlocking breakthrough ideas?
Here's a summary:

1.	Design a stellar GAME
2.	Build a champion TEAM
3.	Provide TOOLS for success
4.	Imagine your WOWs
5.	PROTOTYPE the essentials
6.	Collect detailed FEEDBACK
7.	ITERATE and improve

And then, before signing off, include
a little something extra.

As if dessert weren't enough,
add a cherry to that sweet, sweet sundae.

Make your solution a WOW PLUS!!!

I hope you've enjoyed our innovation adventure and
are bursting with problem-solving zeal.

But wait, there's more . . .

The Puzzler Company team members are all artist-innovators!
David is a multi-genre pianist and composer. Lance plays euphonium
and sings comedy songs. Beyond drawing, Patti acts and even raps.
And designer Cara is a world-class Flamenco dancer.

Until next time, happy puzzling!

Learn more about our method and madness:

www.thepuzzlercompany.com

■ You have but one shot at the GAME of life.

Take bold steps to ensure yours is a **WOW!**

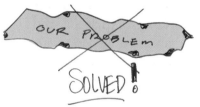

Gratitudes

Teams beat soloists when tackling complex challenges. *The GAME of Innovation* was no exception. We are grateful to the many "creative geniuses" who have participated in our innovation GAMEs, opened up their communities, collaborated on projects, trusted the process, offered feedback, and influenced the methodology. Our approach is exponentially stronger as a result.

To the wonderful colleagues who reviewed this book, thank you for your generous time and suggestions. Each of you played a crucial role in shaping the vision: Renai Albaugh, Ron Beghetto, Warren Berger, Elizabeth Crook, Sabrina Habib, Rob Howell, Alyssa Martina, Ruth Mills, Monica Snellings, Jennifer Snow, Steve Straus, Hildy Teegen, Donna Walker-Kuhne, Patty Wong, Bea Wray. Namaste to agent John Willig for immediately embracing the vision and diving in head first, to editor Donya Dickerson's undying enthusiasm for this monumental project, and to kindred spirit Scott Pardue for his brilliant photography. A Mount Everest–sized bucket of gratitude goes to Tina Cantrell and Erika Cutler, who must have critiqued each sentence six times apiece.

From **David**

I am indebted to my extraordinary family for their love and support, and to Lance, Patti, Cara, and the whole Puzzler team for their unwavering commitment to excellence and exploration.

From **Lance**

Wow, Hannah—Mom Diva'd a race—Patti, bit tape! Patti bit tape, Cara! David, Mom, Hannah—Wow!

From **Patti**

Many thanks to this team of creative geniuses who painstakingly birthed this fantastic user guide. Special thanks to my wife, Julie Boardman, for her loving, supporting adventure-seeking, city-moving self.

From **Cara**

Forever grateful for the phone call that put me on a path with these three extraordinary humans, and for my family and the strength they bestow upon me every day.

Finally, we tip our proverbial steampunk hat to you, the reader, for being active accomplices to positive change. During this complicated and wonderful time, the world is fortunate to have visionaries like you with the courage—and audacity—to innovate the future.

Index

For further reading and resources, visit:

www.thepuzzlercompany.com/resources

For a summary of acronyms, alliterations, and approaches introduced in this book, visit:

www.thepuzzlercompany.com/approaches

Meet the Team

Lance LaDuke Contributor

"My hope is not to predict the future, but to embrace tools, clues, and allies that lead us there (while enjoying some laughs along the way)."

Teacher, creator, futurist, and performer Lance LaDuke has engaged audiences in all 50 states and 25 countries, sharing ideas on technology, problem solving, the arts, and entrepreneurship.

Patti Dobrowolski Illustrator

"A simple picture will change everything! (Even if you can't draw . . .)"

Patti Dobrowolski uses visuals and creative processes to help companies and individuals around the world accelerate growth and change. A critically acclaimed comic performer, keynote speaker, writer, and business consultant, she has brought innovative visual practices to Fortune 500 companies, NGOs, and small businesses. Her consulting career spans 25 years, working to design, develop, and facilitate workshops with all levels of organizations across multiple industries.

Cara Belloso Pinto Designer

"Contrast, in design and life, makes every day more interesting."

Graphic designer by day, flamenco dancer by night, Cara Belloso was born in Caracas, Venezuela. Since moving to the United States in 1994, she has designed for CNN en Español, TNT Latin America, the Coca-Cola Company, and many other organizations.

David Cutler Author

"If 1,000 people consider a particular challenge, and 999 spot roadblocks, I aspire to be the one who sees things differently."

Speaker, author, consultant, and facilitator David Cutler is known for leading immersive "innovation GAMEs." These powerful, team-based experiences have empowered business, arts, and education communities from around the globe to solve creative challenges while becoming better collaborators. He is also an award-winning, multi-genre musician and Yamaha Master Educator. Dr. Cutler is a Distinguished Professor at University of South Carolina, where he teaches innovation and entrepreneurship, and a member of the Liberty Fellowship and Aspen Global Leadership Network.